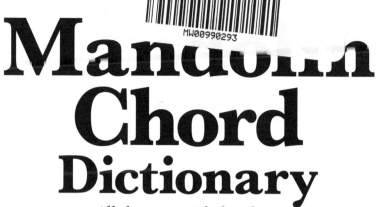

Mandolin
Chord
Dictionary

All the essential chords in
an easy-to-follow format!

Alfred Music Co., Inc.
P.O. Box 10003
Van Nuys, CA 91410-0003
alfred.com

Copyright © MMXVI by Alfred Music Co., Inc.
All rights reserved. Printed in USA.

ISBN-10: 1-4706-2052-9
ISBN-13: 978-1-4706-2052-3

Cover Photo
Gibson mandolin courtesy of Gibson USA.

 Alfred Cares. Contents printed on environmentally responsible paper.

Contents

Introduction

Alfred's Mini Music Guide *Mandolin Chord Dictionary* provides
the most essential chords and chordal information in a portable,
handy size and is loaded with a variety of fingerings for the most
important chords in all 12 keys.

Starting on page 22, the chords are listed alphabetically and
chromatically for quick reference (A♭, A, B♭, B, etc.). On each page,
the chord fingerings are arranged in order from the lowest position
on the fingerboard to the highest. Within each key, chords progress
from the most basic major and minor chords all the way up to 7ths,
9ths, and even altered chords.

For every chord, there is an illustrated chord diagram with
fingerings and note names—see pages 19–20 for an explanation on
how to read these.

The first part of this book (pages 5–14) helps you understand
intervals and how chords are constructed. Theory on triads, 7th
chords, extended chords, altered chords, and other chord types are
also included.

The Moveable Chords section (starting on page 214) will maximize
your knowledge by showing you how to play 12 different chords
with one single fingering. Once you understand basic chord theory
and the concept of moveable chords, you can take the chords in
this book and use them to fit any performance situation. *Mandolin
Chord Dictionary* provides the foundation for an ever-growing chord
vocabulary that can be applied to all musical styles.

Chord Theory

Intervals

Play any note on the mandolin, then play a note one fret above it. The distance between these two notes is a *half step*. Play another note followed by a note two frets above it. The distance between these two notes is a *whole step* (two half steps). The distance between any two notes is referred to as an *interval*.

In the example below of the C Major scale, the letter names are shown above the notes, and the *scale degrees* (numbers) of the notes are written below. Notice that C is the first degree of the scale, D is the second, etc.

The name of an interval is determined by counting the number of scale degrees from one note to the next. For example, an interval of a 3rd, starting on C, would be determined by counting up three scale degrees, or C–D–E (1–2–3). C to E is a 3rd. An interval of a 4th, starting on C, would be determined by counting up four scale degrees, or C–D–E–F (1–2–3–4). C to F is a 4th.

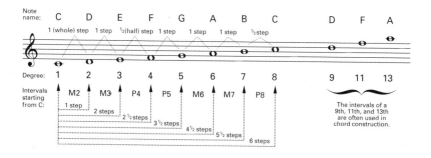

As you can see in last the example, intervals are not only labeled by the distance between scale degrees but by the *quality* of the interval. An interval's quality is determined by counting the number of whole steps and half steps between the two notes of an interval. For example, C to E is a 3rd. C to E is also a *major* 3rd because there are two whole steps between C and E. Likewise, C to E♭ is a 3rd, but C to E♭ is also a *minor* 3rd because there are 1½ steps between C and E♭. There are five qualities used to describe intervals: *major, minor, perfect, diminished,* and *augmented*.

Abbreviations or symbols are used to represent interval qualities:

Abbreviation/ Symbol	Quality
M	Major
m	Minor
P	Perfect
o	Diminished (dim)
+	Augmented (aug)

Particular intervals are associated with certain qualities:

Intervals	Qualities
2nds, 9ths	Major, Minor, and Augmented
3rds, 6ths, 13ths	Major, Minor, Augmented, and Diminished
4ths, 5ths, 11ths	Perfect, Augmented, and Diminished
7ths	Major, Minor, and Diminished

When a major interval is made *smaller* by a half step, it becomes a *minor* interval.

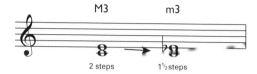

When a minor interval is made *larger* by a half step, it becomes a *major* interval.

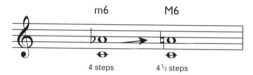

When a minor or perfect interval is made *smaller* by a half step, it becomes a *diminished* interval.

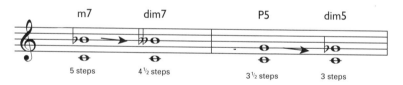

When a major or perfect interval is made *larger* by a half step, it becomes an *augmented* interval.

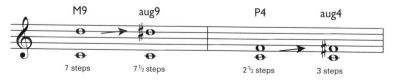

Below is a table of intervals starting on the note C. Notice some intervals are labeled *enharmonic*, which means they are written differently but sound the same (see aug2 and m3).

Table of Intervals

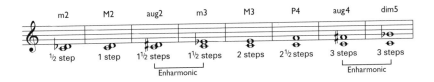

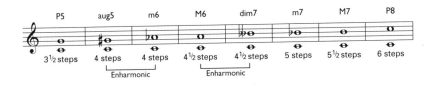

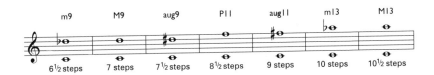

Basic Triads

A *chord* consists of two or more notes played together. Most commonly, a chord will have three or more notes. A three-note chord is called a *triad*. The *root* of a triad (or any other chord) is the note from which a chord is constructed. The relationship of the intervals from the root to the other notes of a chord determines the chord *type*. Triads are most frequently identified as one of four chord types: *major, minor, diminished,* and *augmented.*

All chord types can be identified by the intervals used to create the chord. For example, the C Major triad is built beginning with C as the root, adding a major 3rd (E) and a perfect 5th (G). All major triads contain a root, M3, and P5.

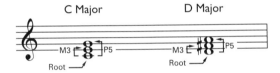

Minor triads contain a root, minor 3rd, and perfect 5th. (An easier way to build a minor triad is to simply lower the 3rd of a major triad.) All minor triads contain a root, m3, and P5.

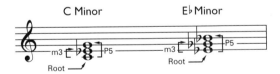

Diminished triads contain a root, minor 3rd, and diminished 5th. If the perfect 5th of a minor triad is made smaller by a half step (to become a diminished 5th), the result is a diminished triad. All diminished triads contain a root, m3, and dim5.

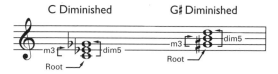

Augmented triads contain a root, major 3rd, and augmented 5th. If the perfect 5th of a major triad is made larger by a half step (to become an augmented 5th), the result is an augmented triad. All augmented triads contain a root, M3, and aug5.

An important concept to remember about chords is that the bottom note of a chord will *not* always be the root. If the root of a triad is moved above the 5th, so that the 3rd is the bottom note of the chord, the chord is in *first inversion*. If the root and 3rd are moved above the 5th, the chord is in *second inversion*. The number of inversions that a chord can have is related to the number of notes in the chord: a three-note chord can have two inversions, a four-note chord can have three inversions, etc.

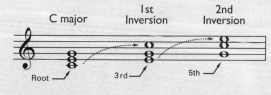

Building Chords

By using the four chord types as basic building blocks, it is possible to create a variety of chords by adding 6ths, 7ths, 9ths, and even 11ths and 13ths. Following are examples of some of the many variations.

*The suspended 4th chord does not contain a 3rd. An assumption is made that the fourth degree of the chord will harmonically resolve to the third degree. In other words, the 4th is suspended until it moves to the 3rd.

Up until now, the examples have featured intervals and chord construction based on C. Until you are familiar with other chords, the examples in C can serve as a reference guide for building chords based on other notes. For instance, locate C7(♭9). To construct a G7(♭9) chord, let's first determine what intervals are contained in C7(♭9).

C Seventh Flat Ninth
C7(♭9)

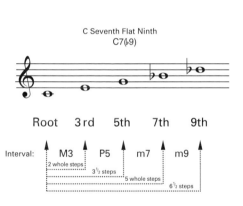

C Seventh Flat Ninth
C7(♭9)

Now, let's figure out how to construct a G7(♭9) chord:

1. Determine the root of the chord. A chord is always named for its root—in this case, G is the root of G7(♭9).

2. Count letter names up from the letter name of the root (G), as we did when building intervals on page 5, to determine the intervals of the chord. Counting three letter names up from G to B (G–A–B, 1–2–3) is a 3rd, G to D (G–A–B–C–D) is a 5th, G to F is a 7th, and G to A is a 9th.

3. Determine the quality of the intervals by counting whole steps and half steps up from the root; G to B (2 whole steps) is a major 3rd, G to D (3½ steps) is a perfect 5th, G to F (5 whole steps) is a minor 7th, and G to A♭ (6½ steps) is a minor 9th.

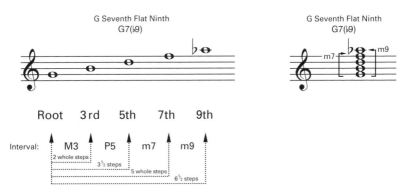

Follow this general guideline to figure out the notes of any chord. As interval and chord construction become more familiar, it will become possible to create your own original fingerings on the mandolin. Feel free to experiment!

The Circle of 5ths

Mandolin Chord Dictionary is organized to provide fingerings for chords in all keys. The *circle of 5ths* below will help clarify which chords are enharmonic equivalents (notice that chords can be written enharmonically as well, see page 8). The circle of 5ths also serves as a quick reference guide to the relationship of the keys and how *key signatures* can be figured out. (A key signature, which indicates the key, is a group of sharps or flats at the beginning of a staff. Note that the key signature for C has no sharps or flats.) Clockwise movement (up a P5) provides all of the sharp keys by adding one sharp to the key signature. Moving counterclockwise (down a P5) provides the flat keys by adding one flat.

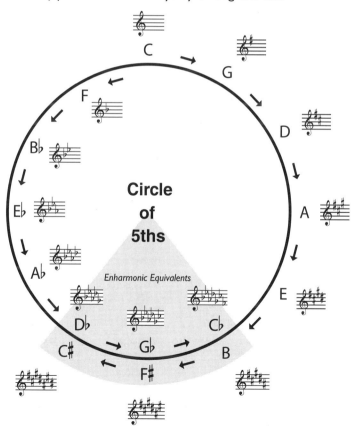

Circle of 5ths

Enharmonic Equivalents

Reading Chords

Chord Symbol Variations

A *chord symbol* is a musical shorthand that gives mandolin players as much information about a chord as quickly as possible. Since chord symbols are not universally standardized, they are often written in many different ways—some are understandable, others might be confusing. To illustrate this point, following are some of the various ways music copyists, composers, and arrangers have notated common chords.

C	Csus	C($\flat$5)	C(add9)
C major Cmaj CM	Csus4 C(addF) C4	C-5 C(5-) C($\sharp$4)	C(9) C(add2) C(+9) C(+D)
C5	**Cm**	**C+**	**C°**
C(no3) C(omit3)	Cmin Cmi C-	C+5 Caug Caug5 C($\sharp$5)	C° C°7 C7°
C6	**C6/9**	**Cm6/9**	**Cm6**
Cmaj6 C(addA) C(A)	C6(add9) C6(addD) C9(no7) C9/6	C-6/9 Cm6(+9) Cm6(add9) Cm6(+D)	C-6 Cm(addA) Cm(+6)

C7	C7sus	Cm7	Cm7($\flat$5)
C(addB$\flat$)	C7sus4	Cmi7	Cmi7-5
C7̵	Csus7	Omin7	C-7(5-)
C(-7)	C7(+4)	C-7	C⊖
C(+7)		C7mi	C ½dim

C7+	C7($\flat$5)	Cmaj7	Cmaj7($\flat$5)
C7+5	C7-5	Cma7	Cmaj7(-5)
C7aug	C7(5-)	C7	C7̵(-5)
C7aug5	C7̵-5	C△	C△($\flat$5)
C7($\sharp$5)	C7($\sharp$4)	C△7	

Cm(maj7)	C7($\flat$9)	C7($\sharp$9)	C7+($\flat$9)
C-maj7	C7(-9)	C7(+9)	Caug7-9
C-7̵	C9$\flat$	C9$\sharp$	C+7($\flat$9)
Cmi7̵	C9-	C9+	C+9$\flat$
			C7+(-9)

Cm9	C9	C9+	C9($\flat$5)
Cm7(9)	C$_7^9$	C9(+5)	C9(-5)
Cm7(+9)	C7add9	Caug9	C7$_{-5}^9$
C-9	C7(addD)	C(9#5)	C9(5$\flat$)
Cmi7(9+)	C7(+9)	C+9	

Cmaj9	C9(#11)	Cm9(maj7)	C11
C$\overline{7}$(9)	C9(+11)	C-9(#$\overline{7}$)	C9(11)
C$\overline{7}$(+9)	C(#11)	C(-9)$\overline{7}$	C9addF
C9(maj7)	C11+	Cmi9(#$\overline{7}$)	C9+11
C$\overline{9}$	C11#		C7$_{11}^9$

Cm11	C13	C13($\flat$9)	C13($^{\flat 9}_{\flat 5}$)
C-11	C9addA	C13(-9)	C13(-9-5)
Cm(11)	C9(6)	C$_{\flat 9}^{13}$	C($\flat$9$\flat$5)addA
Cmi7$_9^{11}$	C7addA	C($\flat$9)addA	
C-7($_{11}^9$)	C7+A		

Chord Frames

Mandolin *chord frames* are diagrams that contain all the information needed to play a particular chord. The fingerings, note names, and position of the chord on the neck are all provided in the chord frame. The photo below shows how the fretting-hand fingers are numbered.

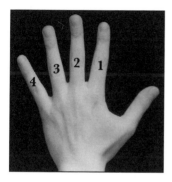

The following illustrations explain the various chord frame symbols.

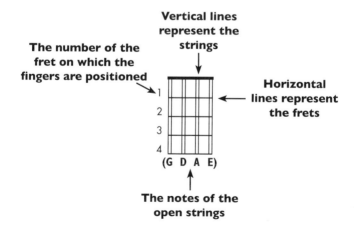

An X indicates that the string is unplayed or muted

Open (unfingered) strings

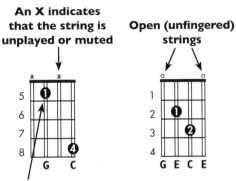

Circles indicate on which fret and which string the finger is placed—the number indicates which finger is used

Slurs indicate that the finger is placed flat, covering the marked notes

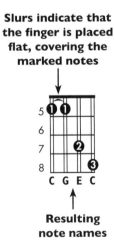

Resulting note names

Choosing Chord Positions

For smoother and more comfortable transitions between chords in a progression, choose chord positions that require the least motion from one chord to the next. Use fingerings that are in approximately the same area of the mandolin neck.

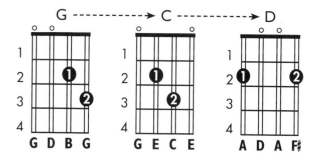

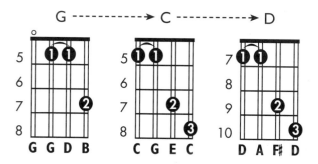

Chords in All 12 Keys

A♭

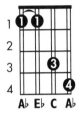

Ab Eb C Ab

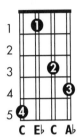

C Eb C Ab

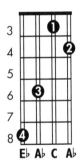

Eb Ab C Ab

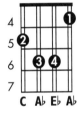

C Ab Eb Ab

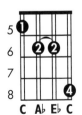

C Ab Eb C

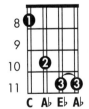

C Ab Eb Ab

A♭m

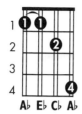

A♭ E♭ C♭ A♭

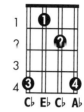

C♭ E♭ C♭ A♭

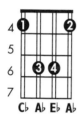

C♭ A♭ E♭ A♭

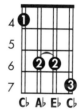

C♭ A♭ E♭ C♭

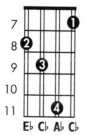

E♭ C♭ A♭ C♭

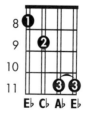

E♭ C♭ A♭ E♭

A♭°

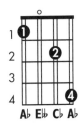

A♭ E♭♭ C♭ A♭

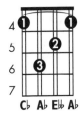

C♭ A♭ E♭♭ A♭

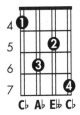

C♭ A♭ E♭♭ C♭

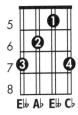

E♭♭ A♭ E♭♭ C♭

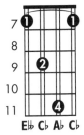

E♭♭ C♭ A♭ C♭

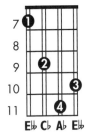

E♭♭ C♭ A♭ E♭♭

A♭+

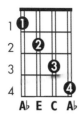

A♭ E C A♭

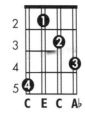

C E C A♭

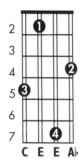

C E E A♭

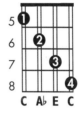

C A♭ E C

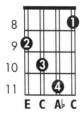

E C A♭ C

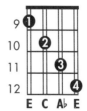

E C A♭ E

A♭5

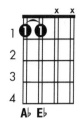

A♭ E♭

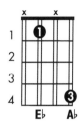

E♭ A♭

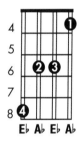

E♭ A♭ E♭ A♭

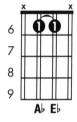

A♭ E♭

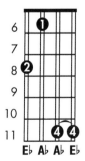

E♭ A♭ A♭ E♭

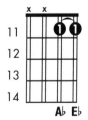

A♭ E♭

A♭sus4

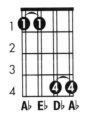

A♭ E♭ D♭ A♭

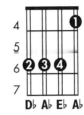

D♭ A♭ E♭ A♭

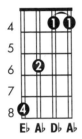

E♭ A♭ D♭ A♭

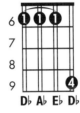

D♭ A♭ E♭ D♭

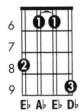

E♭ A♭ E♭ D♭

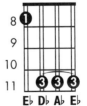

E♭ D♭ A♭ E♭

A♭6

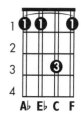

Ab Eb C F

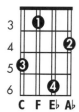

C F Eb Ab

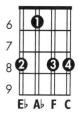

Eb Ab F C

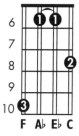

F Ab Eb C

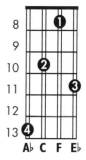

Ab C F Eb

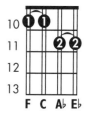

F C Ab Eb

A♭m6

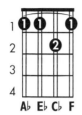

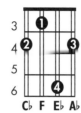

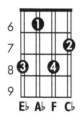

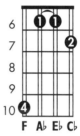

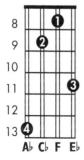

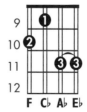

A♭maj7

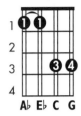

A♭ E♭ C G

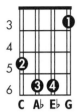

C A♭ E♭ G

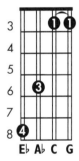

E♭ A♭ C G

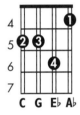

C G E♭ A♭

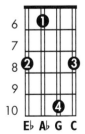

E♭ A♭ G C

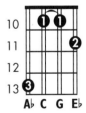

A♭ C G E♭

A♭7

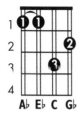

1 2 3 4

A♭ E♭ C G♭

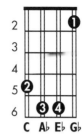

2 3 4 5 6

C A♭ E♭ G♭

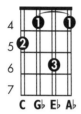

4 5 6 7

C G♭ E♭ A♭

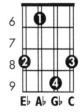

6 7 8 9

E♭ A♭ G♭ C

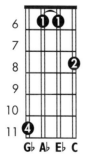

6 7 8 9 10 11

G♭ A♭ E♭ C

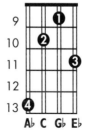

9 10 11 12 13

A♭ C G♭ E♭

A♭m7

A♭

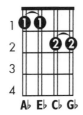

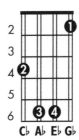

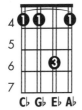

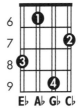

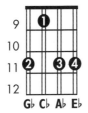

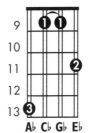

A♭m7(♭5)

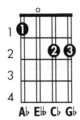

A♭ E♭♭ C♭ G♭

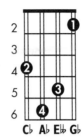

C♭ A♭ E♭♭ G♭

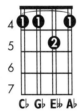

C♭ G♭ E♭♭ A♭

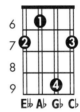

E♭♭ A♭ G♭ C♭

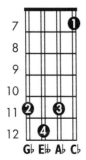

G♭ E♭♭ A♭ C♭

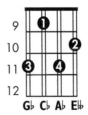

G♭ C♭ A♭ E♭♭

Ab°7

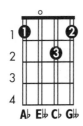

Ab Ebb Cb Gbb

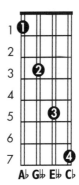

Ab Gbb Ebb Cb

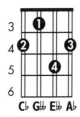

Cb Gbb Ebb Ab

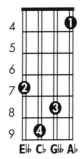

Ebb Cb Gbb Ab

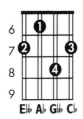

Ebb Ab Gbb Cb

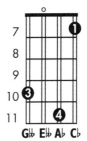

Gbb Ebb Ab Cb

A♭(add9)

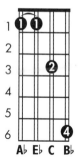

A♭ E♭ C B♭

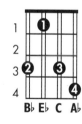

B♭ E♭ C A♭

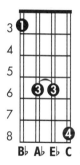

B♭ A♭ E♭ C

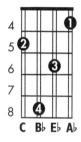

C B♭ E♭ A♭

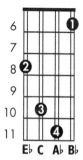

E♭ C A♭ B♭

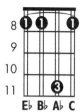

E♭ B♭ A♭ C

A♭maj9

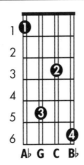
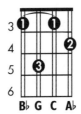

A♭9

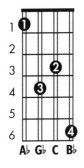
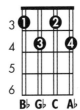

A♭m9

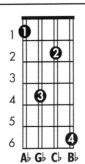
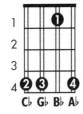

A♭

A♭7+

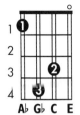

Ab Gb C E

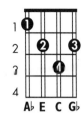

Ab E C Gb

A♭7(♭9)

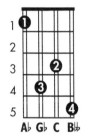

Ab Gb C B♭♭

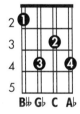

B♭♭ Gb C Ab

A♭7(♯9)

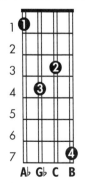

Ab Gb C B

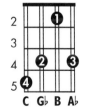

C Gb B Ab

A

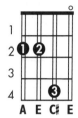

A E C♯ E

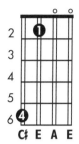

C♯ E A E

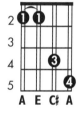

A E C♯ A

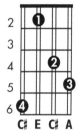

C♯ E C♯ A

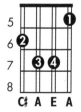

C♯ A E A

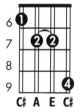

C♯ A E C♯

Am

A E C E

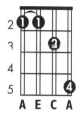

A E C A

A

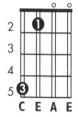

C E A E

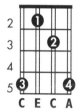

C E C A

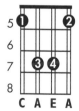

C A E A

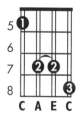

C A E C

A°

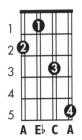

A Eb C A

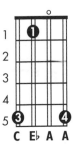

C Eb A A

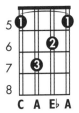

C A Eb A

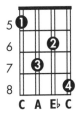

C A Eb C

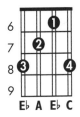

Eb A Eb C

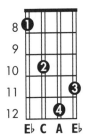

Eb C A Eb

A+

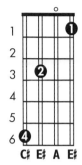

C# E# A E#

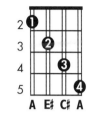

A E# C# A

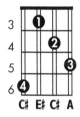

C# E# C# A

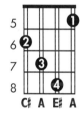

C# A E# A

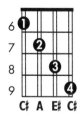

C# A E# C#

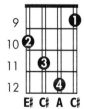

E# C# A C#

A

A5

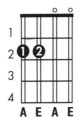

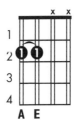

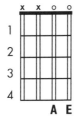

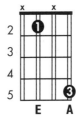

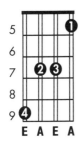

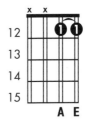

Asus4

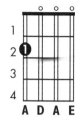

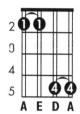

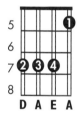

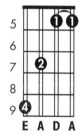

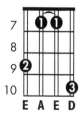

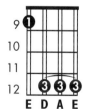

A6

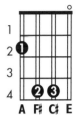
A F# C# E

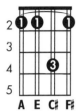
A E C# F#

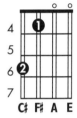
C# F# A E

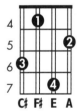
C# F# E A

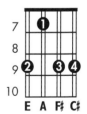
E A F# C#

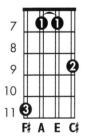
F# A E C#

Am6

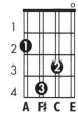

A F# C E

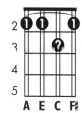

A E C F#

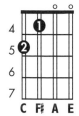

C F# A E

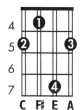

C F# E A

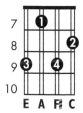

E A F# C

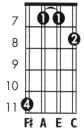

F# A E C

Amaj7

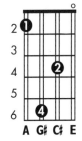

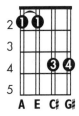

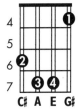

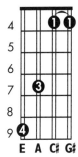

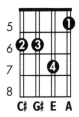

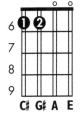

A7

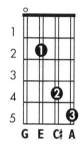

G E C# A

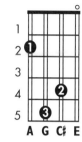

A G C# E

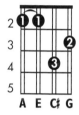

A E C# G

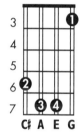

C# A E G

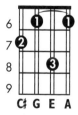

C# G E A

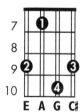

E A G C#

Am7

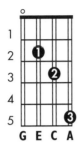

G E C A

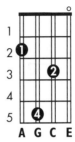

A G C E

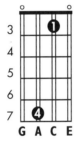

G A C E

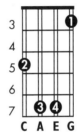

C A E G

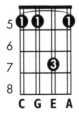

C G E A

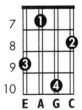

E A G C

Am7(♭5)

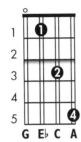

G E♭ C A

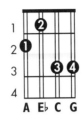

A E♭ C G

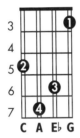

C A E♭ G

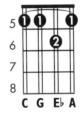

C G E♭ A

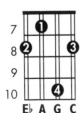

E♭ A G C

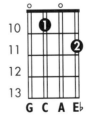

G C A E♭

A

A°7

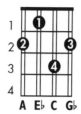

A Eb C Gb

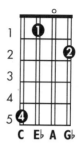

C Eb A Gb

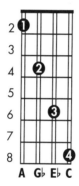

A Gb Eb C

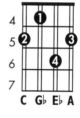

C Gb Eb A

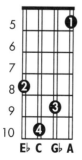

Eb C Gb A

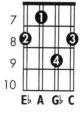

Eb A Gb C

A(add9)

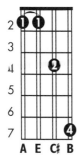

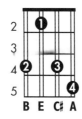

A

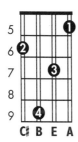

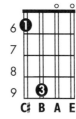

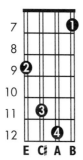

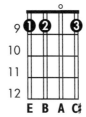

Amaj9

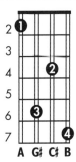

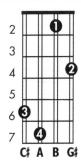

A9

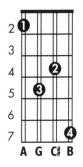

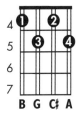

Am9

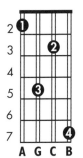

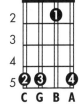

A

A7+

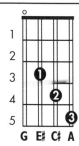

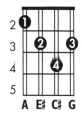

A7(♭9)

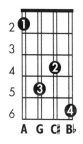

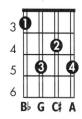

A7(♯9)

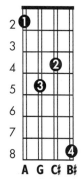

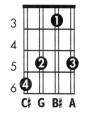

B♭

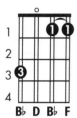

B♭ D B♭ F

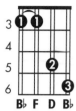

B♭ F D B♭

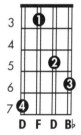

D F D B♭

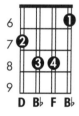

D B♭ F B♭

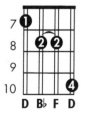

D B♭ F D

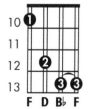

F D B♭ F

B♭m

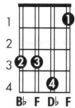

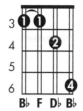

B♭

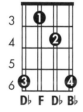

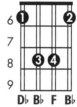

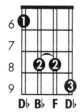

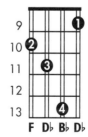

B♭°

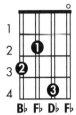

B♭ F♭ D♭ F♭

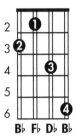

B♭ F♭ D♭ B♭

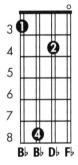

B♭ B♭ D♭ F♭

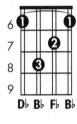

D♭ B♭ F♭ B♭

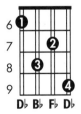

D♭ B♭ F♭ D♭

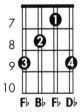

F♭ B♭ F♭ D♭

B♭

B♭+

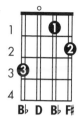

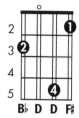

B♭

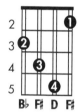

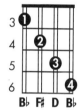

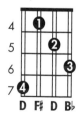

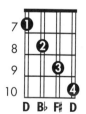

B♭5

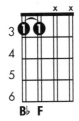

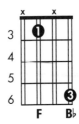

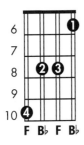

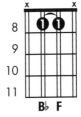

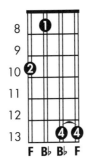

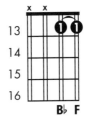

B♭sus4

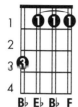

B♭ E♭ B♭ F

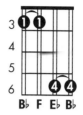

B♭ F E♭ B♭

B♭

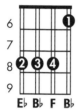

E♭ B♭ F B♭

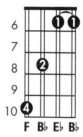

F B♭ E♭ B♭

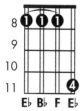

E♭ B♭ F E♭

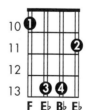

F E♭ B♭ E♭

B♭6

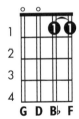

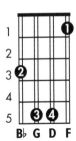

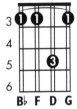

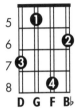

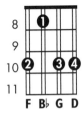

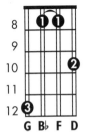

B♭m6

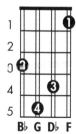

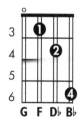

B♭

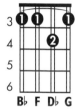

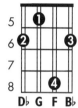

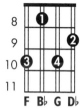

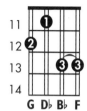

B♭maj7

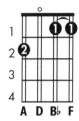

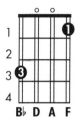

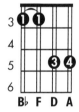

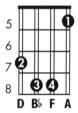

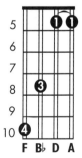

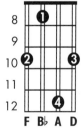

B♭7

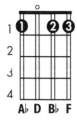

A♭ D B♭ F

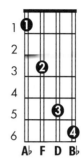

A♭ F D B♭

B♭

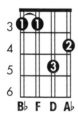

B♭ F D A♭

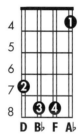

D B♭ F A♭

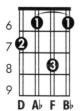

D A♭ F B♭

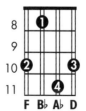

F B♭ A♭ D

B♭m7

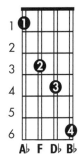

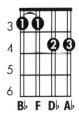

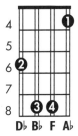

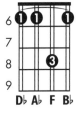

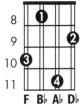

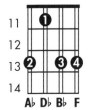

B♭m7(♭5)

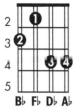

B♭ F♭ D♭ A♭

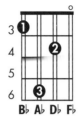

B♭ A♭ D♭ F♭

B♭

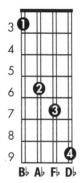

B♭ A♭ F♭ D♭

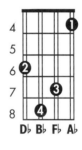

D♭ B♭ F♭ A♭

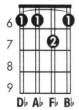

D♭ A♭ F♭ B♭

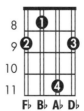

F♭ B♭ A♭ D♭

B♭°7

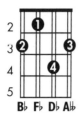

B♭ F♭ D♭ A♭♭

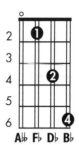

A♭♭ F♭ D♭ B♭

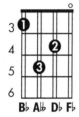

B♭ A♭♭ D♭ F♭

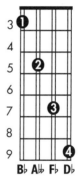

B♭ A♭♭ F♭ D♭

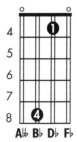

A♭♭ B♭ D♭ F♭

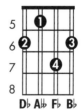

D♭ A♭♭ F♭ B♭

B♭(add9)

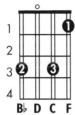

B♭ D C F

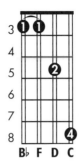

B♭ F D C

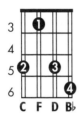

C F D B♭

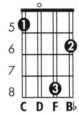

C D F B♭

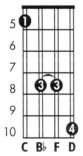

C B♭ F D

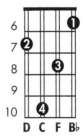

D C F B♭

B♭

B♭maj9

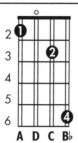

A D C B♭

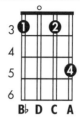

B♭ D C A

B♭9

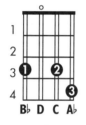

B♭ D C A♭

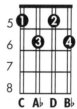

C A♭ D B♭

B♭m9

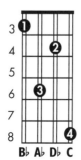

B♭ A♭ D♭ C

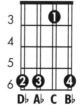

D♭ A♭ C B♭

B♭7+

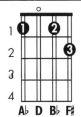

A♭ D B♭ F#

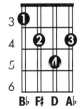

B♭ F# D A♭

B♭

B♭7(♭9)

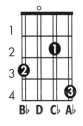

B♭ D C♭ A♭

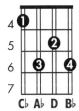

C♭ A♭ D B♭

B♭7(#9)

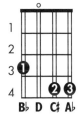

B♭ D C# A♭

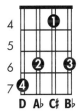

D A♭ C# B♭

B

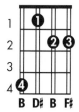

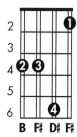

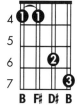

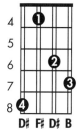

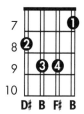

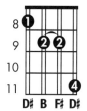

Bm

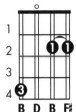

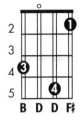

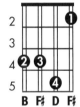

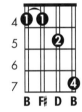

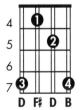

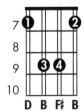

B°

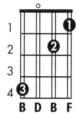

B D B F

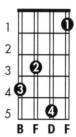

B F D F

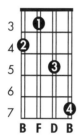

B F D B

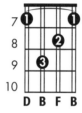

D B F B

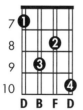

D B F D

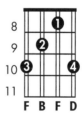

F B F D

B+

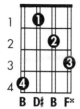

B D# B F×

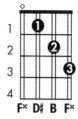

F× D# B F×

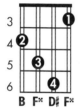

B F× D# F×

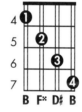

B F× D# B

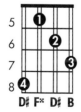

D# F× D# B

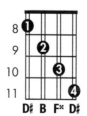

D# B F× D#

B

B5

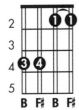

2
3
4 ❸ ❹
5
B F♯ B F♯

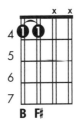

4 ❶ ❶
5
6
7
B F♯

B

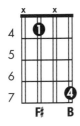

4 ❶
5
6
7 ❹
F♯ B

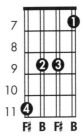

7 ❶
8
9 ❷ ❸
10
11 ❹
F♯ B F♯ B

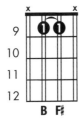

9 ❶ ❶
10
11
12
B F♯

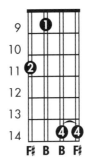

9 ❶
10
11 ❷
12
13
14 ❹ ❹
F♯ B B F♯

Bsus4

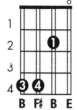

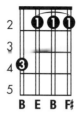

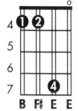

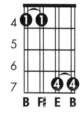

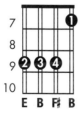

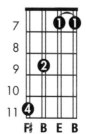

B

B6

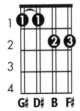

G# D# B F#

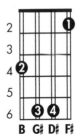

B G# D# F#

B

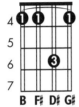

B F# D# G#

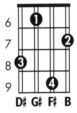

D# G# F# B

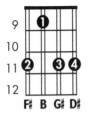

F# B G# D#

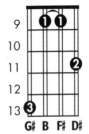

G# B F# D#

Bm6

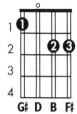

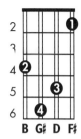

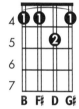

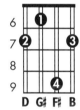

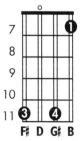

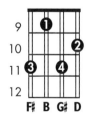

B

Bmaj7

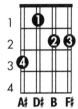

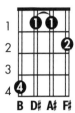

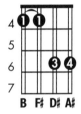

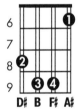

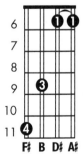

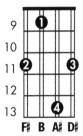

B7

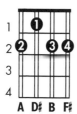

A D# B F#

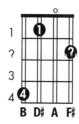

B D# A F#

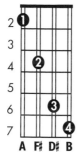

A F# D# B

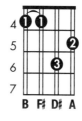

B F# D# A

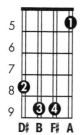

D# B F# A

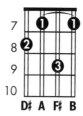

D# A F# B

Bm7

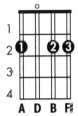

A D B F#

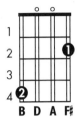

B D A F#

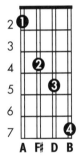

A F# D B

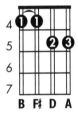

B F# D A

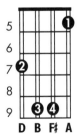

D B F# A

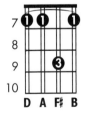

D A F# B

Bm7(♭5)

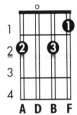

A D B F

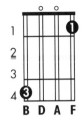

B D A F

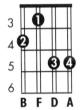

B F D A

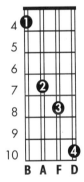

B A F D

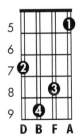

D B F A

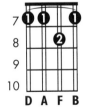

D A F B

B

B°7

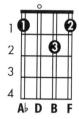

A♭ D B F

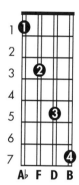

A♭ F D B

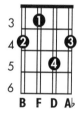

B F D A♭

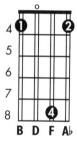

B D F A♭

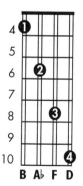

B A♭ F D

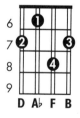

D A♭ F B

B(add9)

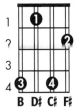

1
2
3
4

B D♯ C♯ F♯

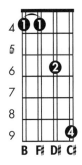

4
5
6
7
8
9

B F♯ D♯ C♯

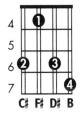

4
5
6
7

C♯ F♯ D♯ B

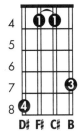

4
5
6
7
8

D♯ F♯ C♯ B

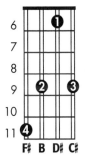

6
7
8
9
10
11

F♯ B D♯ C♯

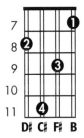

7
8
9
10
11

D♯ C♯ F♯ B

B

Bmaj9

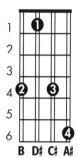

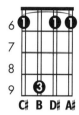

B9

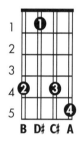

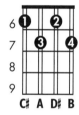

Bm9

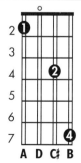

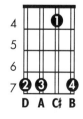

B7+

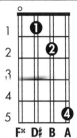

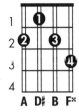

B7(♭9)

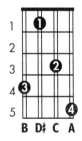

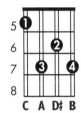

B7(♯9)

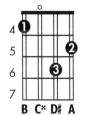

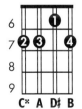

C

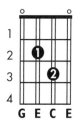

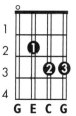

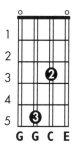

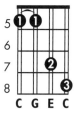

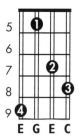

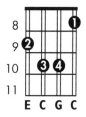

Cm

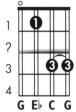

G Eb C G

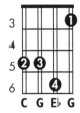

C G Eb G

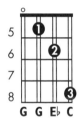

G G Eb C

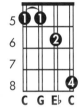

C G Eb C

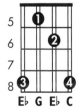

Eb G Eb C

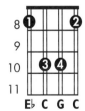

Eb C G C

C

87

C°

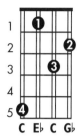

C Eb C Gb

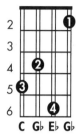

C Gb Eb Gb

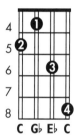

C Gb Eb C

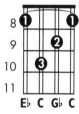

Eb C Gb C

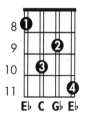

Eb C Gb Eb

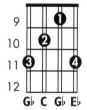

Gb C Gb Eb

C+

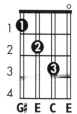

G# E C E

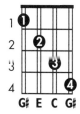

G# E C G#

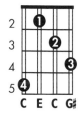

C E C G#

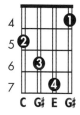

C G# E G#

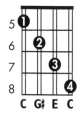

C G# E C

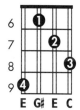

E G# E C

C

C5

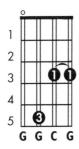

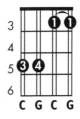

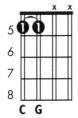

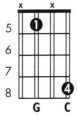

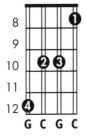

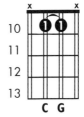

Csus4

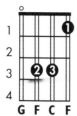

G F C F

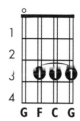

G F C G

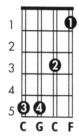

C G C F

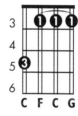

C F C G

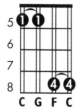

C G F C

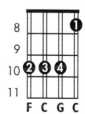

F C G C

C

C6

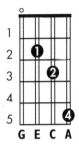

G E C A

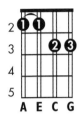

A E C G

C

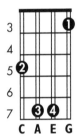

C A E G

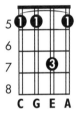

C G E A

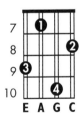

E A G C

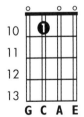

G C A E

92

Cm6

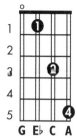

G Eb C A

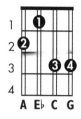

A Eb C G

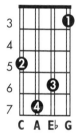

C A Eb G

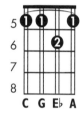

C G Eb A

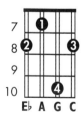

Eb A G C

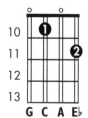

G C A Eb

C

Cmaj7

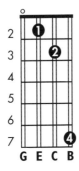

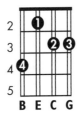

C

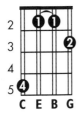

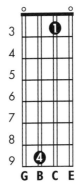

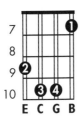

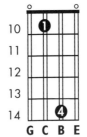

C7

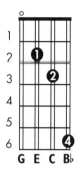

G E C B♭

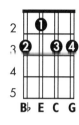

B♭ E C G

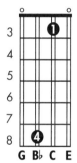

G B♭ C E

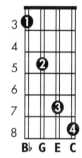

B♭ G E C

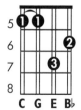

C G E B♭

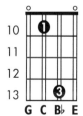

G C B♭ E

C

Cm7

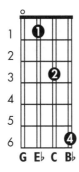

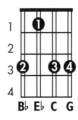

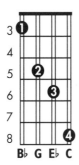

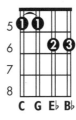

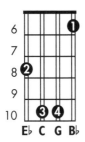

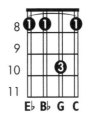

96

Cm7(♭5)

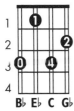

B♭ E♭ C G♭

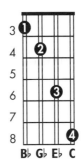

B♭ G♭ E♭ C

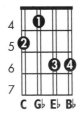

C G♭ E♭ B♭

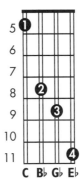

C B♭ G♭ E♭

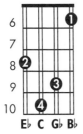

E♭ C G♭ B♭

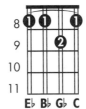

E♭ B♭ G♭ C

C

C°7

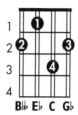

B♭♭ E♭ C G♭

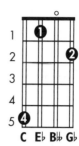

C E♭ B♭♭ G♭

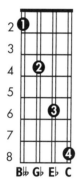

B♭♭ G♭ E♭ C

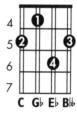

C G♭ E♭ B♭♭

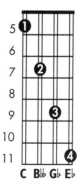

C B♭♭ G♭ E♭

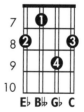

E♭ B♭♭ G♭ C

98

C(add9)

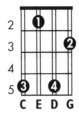

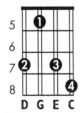

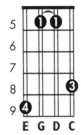

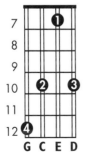

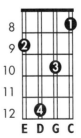

C

Cmaj9

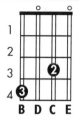

B D C E

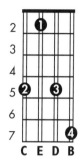

C E D B

C9

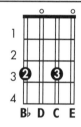

B♭ D C E

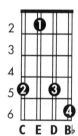

C E D B♭

Cm9

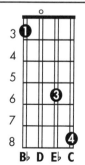

B♭ D E♭ C

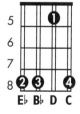

E♭ B♭ D C

C7+

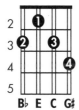

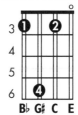

C7(♭9)

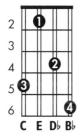

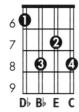

C7(♯9)

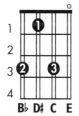

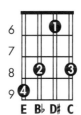

C#

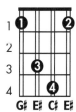

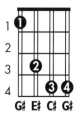

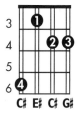

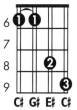

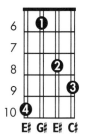

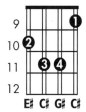

C#m

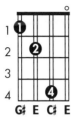

G# E C# E

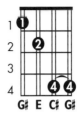

G# E C# G#

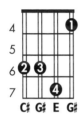

C# G# E G#

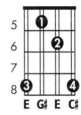

E G# E C#

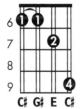

C# G# E C#

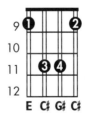

E C# G# C#

C#

C#°

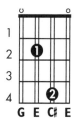

G E C# E

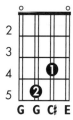

G G C# E

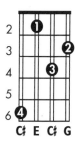

C# E C# G

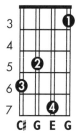

C# G E G

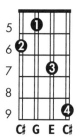

C# G E C#

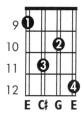

E C# G E

C#+

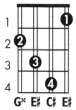

G× E# C# E#

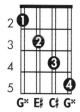

G× E# C# G×

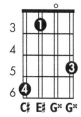

C# E# G× G×

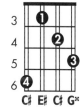

C# E# C# G×

C#

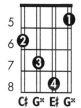

C# G× E# G×

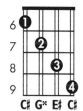

C# G× E# C#

105

C#5

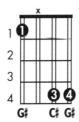

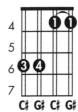

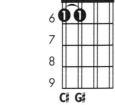

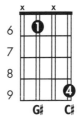

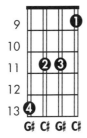

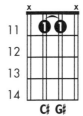

C#

C#sus4

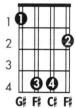

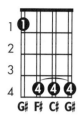

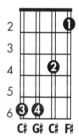

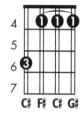

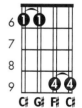

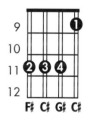

C#

C#6

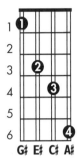

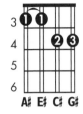

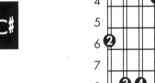

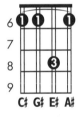

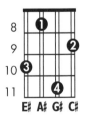

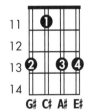

C#m6

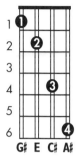

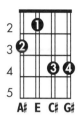

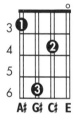

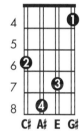

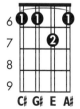

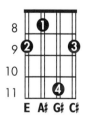

C#

C#maj7

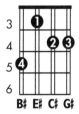

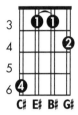

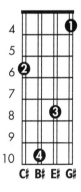

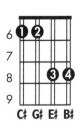

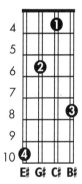

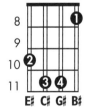

C#7

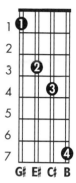

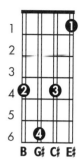

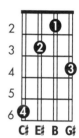

C#

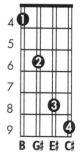

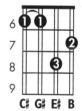

C#m7

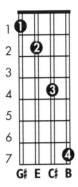

G# E C# B

B E C# G#

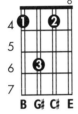

B G# C# E

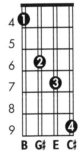

B G# E C#

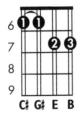

C# G# E B

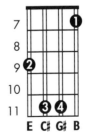

E C# G# B

C#m7(♭5)

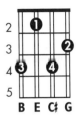

B E C# G

G B C# E

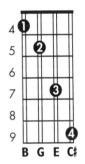

B G E C#

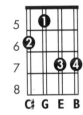

C# G E B

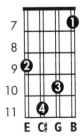

E C# G B

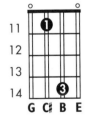

G C# B E

C#

C#°7

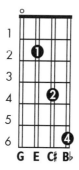

G E C# B♭

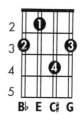

B♭ E C# G

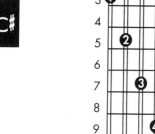

B♭ G E C#

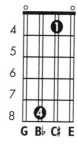

G B♭ C# E

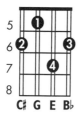

C# G E B♭

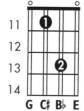

G C# B♭ E

C#

C#(add9)

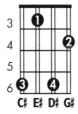

C# E# D# G#

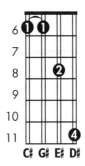

C# G# E# D#

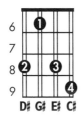

D# G# E# C#

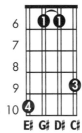

E# G# D# C#

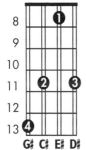

G# C# E# D#

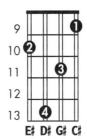

E# D# G# C#

C#

C#maj9

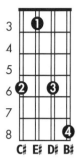

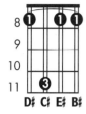

C#9

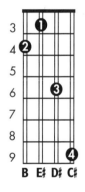

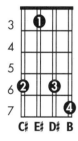

C#m9

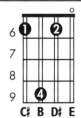

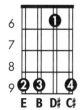

C#

C#7+

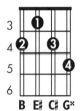

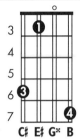

C#7(♭9)

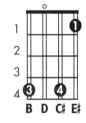

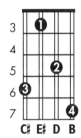

C#7(#9)

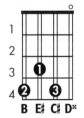

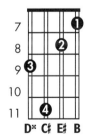

D

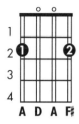

A D A F#

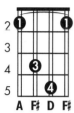

A F# D F#

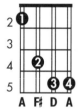

A F# D A

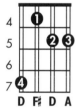

D F# D A

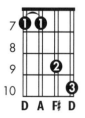

D A F# D

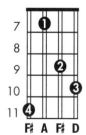

F# A F# D

D

Dm

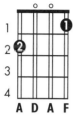

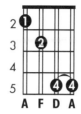

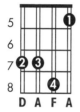

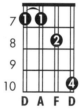

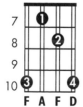

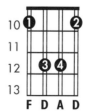

D

119

D°

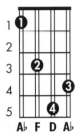

1 2 3 4 5

Ab F D Ab

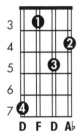

3 4 5 6 7

D F D Ab

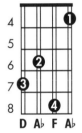

4 5 6 7 8

D Ab F Ab

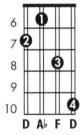

6 7 8 9 10

D Ab F D

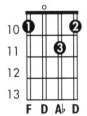

10 11 12 13

F D Ab D

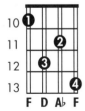

10 11 12 13

F D Ab F

D

120

D+

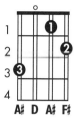

A# D A# F#

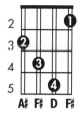

A# F# D F#

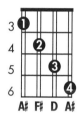

A# F# D A#

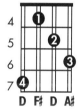

D F# D A#

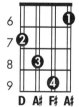

D A# F# A#

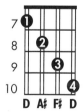

D A# F# D

D

D5

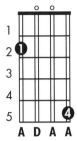

A D A A

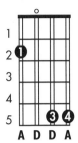

A D D A

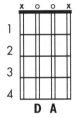

D A

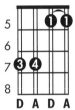

D A D A

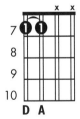

D A

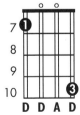

D D A D

D

Dsus4

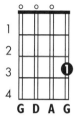

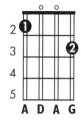

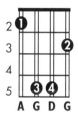

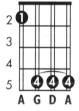

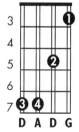

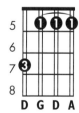

D

D6

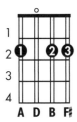

A D B F#

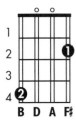

B D A F#

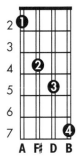

A F# D B

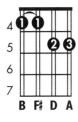

B F# D A

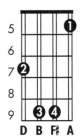

D B F# A

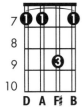

D A F# B

Dm6

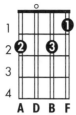

A D B F

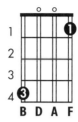

B D A F

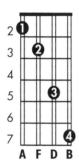

A F D B

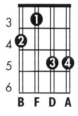

B F D A

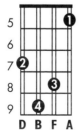

D B F A

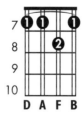

D A F B

D

125

Dmaj7

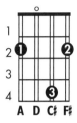

A D C# F#

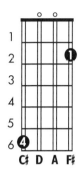

C# D A F#

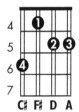

C# F# D A

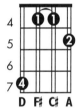

D F# C# A

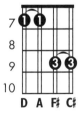

D A F# C#

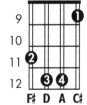

F# D A C#

D7

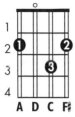

A D C F#

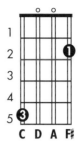

C D A F#

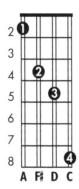

A F# D C

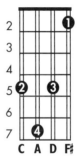

C A D F#

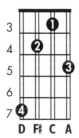

D F# C A

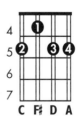

C F# D A

D

Dm7

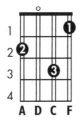

A D C F

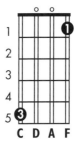

C D A F

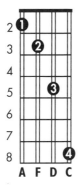

A F D C

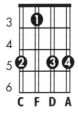

C F D A

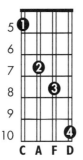

C A F D

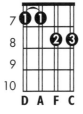

D A F C

D

Dm7(♭5)

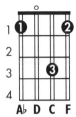

A♭ D C F

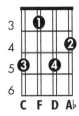

C F D A♭

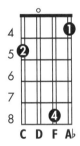

C D F A♭

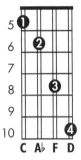

C A♭ F D

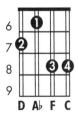

D A♭ F C

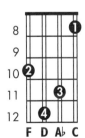

F D A♭ C

D

129

D°7

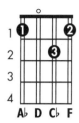

A♭ D C♭ F

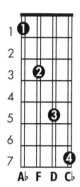

A♭ F D C♭

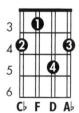

C♭ F D A♭

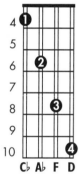

C♭ A♭ F D

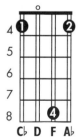

C♭ D F A♭

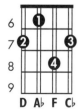

D A♭ F C♭

D

D(add9)

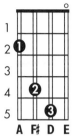

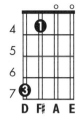

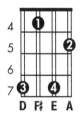

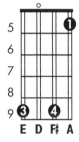

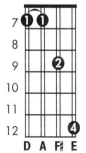

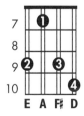

D

Dmaj9

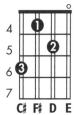

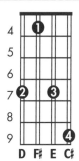

D9

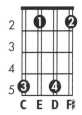

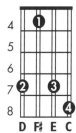

Dm9

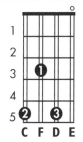

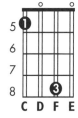

D7+

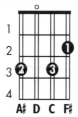

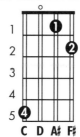

D7(♭9)

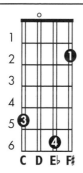

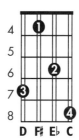

D7(♯9)

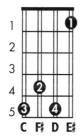

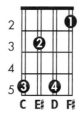

D

E♭

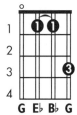

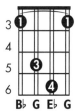

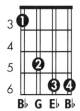

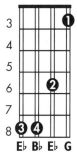

E♭

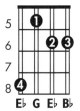

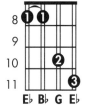

E♭m

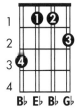

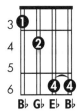

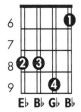

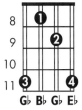

E♭

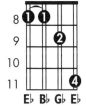

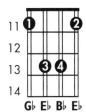

E♭°

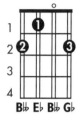

B𝄫 E♭ B𝄫 G♭

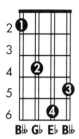

B𝄫 G♭ E♭ B𝄫

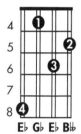

E♭ G♭ E♭ B𝄫

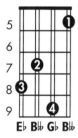

E♭ B𝄫 G♭ B𝄫

E♭

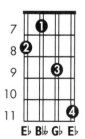

E♭ B𝄫 G♭ E♭

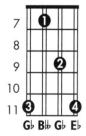

G♭ B𝄫 G♭ E♭

E♭+

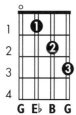

G E♭ B G

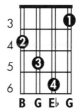

B G E♭ G

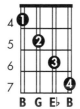

B G E♭ B

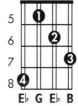

E♭ G E♭ B

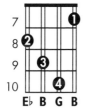

E♭ B G B

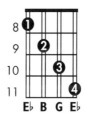

E♭ B G E♭

E♭

E♭5

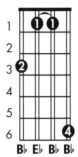

Bb Eb Bb Bb

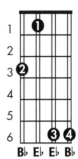

Bb Eb Eb Bb

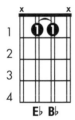

Eb Bb

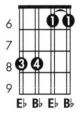

Eb Bb Eb Bb

Eb

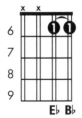

Eb Bb

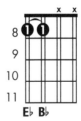

Eb Bb

E♭sus4

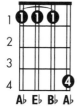

A♭ E♭ B♭ A♭

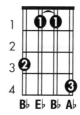

B♭ E♭ B♭ A♭

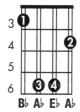

B♭ A♭ E♭ A♭

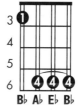

B♭ A♭ E♭ B♭

E♭

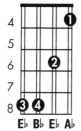

E♭ B♭ E♭ A♭

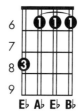

E♭ A♭ E♭ B♭

E♭6

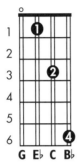

G E♭ C B♭

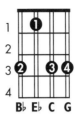

B♭ E♭ C G

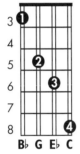

B♭ G E♭ C

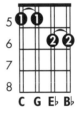

C G E♭ B♭

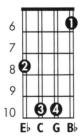

E♭ C G B♭

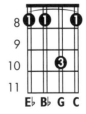

E♭ B♭ G C

E♭

E♭m6

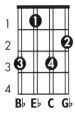

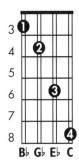

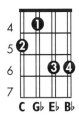

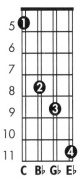

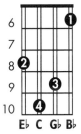

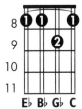

E♭

E♭maj7

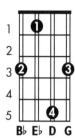

B♭ E♭ D G

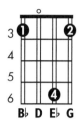

B♭ D E♭ G

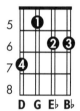

D G E♭ B♭

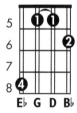

E♭ G D B♭

E♭

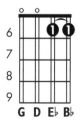

G D E♭ B♭

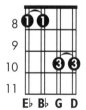

E♭ B♭ G D

E♭7

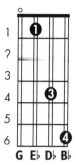

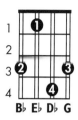

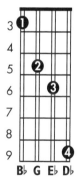

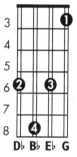

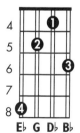

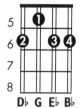

E♭

E♭m7

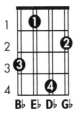

1
2
3
4

B♭ E♭ D♭ G♭

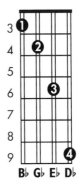

3
4
5
6
7
8
9

B♭ G♭ E♭ D♭

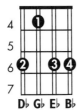

4
5
6
7

D♭ G♭ E♭ B♭

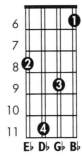

6
7
8
9
10
11

E♭ D♭ G♭ B♭

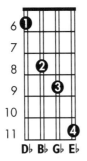

6
7
8
9
10
11

D♭ B♭ G♭ E♭

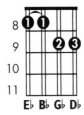

8
9
10
11

E♭ B♭ G♭ D♭

E♭m7(♭5)

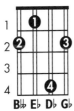

B♭♭ E♭ D♭ G♭

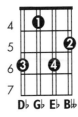

D♭ G♭ E♭ B♭♭

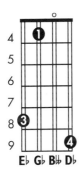

E♭ G♭ B♭♭ D♭

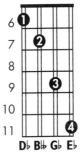

D♭ B♭♭ G♭ E♭

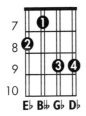

E♭ B♭♭ G♭ D♭

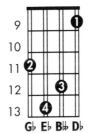

G♭ E♭ B♭♭ D♭

E♭

145

E♭°7

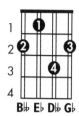

B♭♭ E♭ D♭♭ G♭

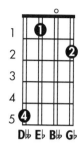

D♭♭ E♭ B♭♭ G♭

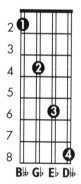

B♭♭ G♭ E♭ D♭♭

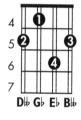

D♭♭ G♭ E♭ B♭♭

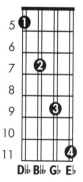

D♭♭ B♭♭ G♭ E♭

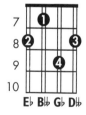

E♭ B♭♭ G♭ D♭♭

E♭

E♭(add9)

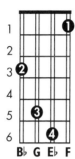

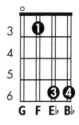

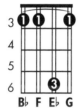

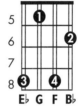

E♭

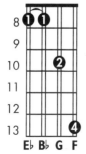

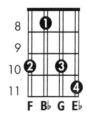

E♭maj9

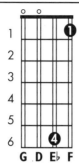

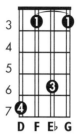

E♭9

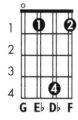

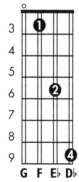

E♭m9

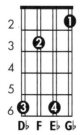

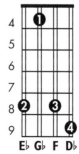

E♭

E♭7+

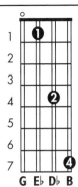

G E♭ D♭ B

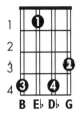

B E♭ D♭ G

E♭7(♭9)

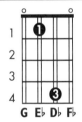

G E♭ D♭ F♭

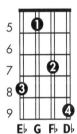

E♭ G F♭ D♭

E♭7(♯9)

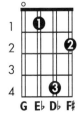

G E♭ D♭ F♯

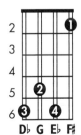

D♭ G E♭ F♯

E

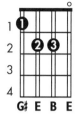

G♯ E B E

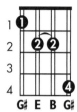

G♯ E B G♯

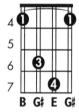

B G♯ E G♯

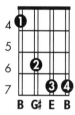

B G♯ E B

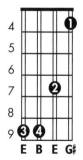

E B E G♯

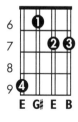

E G♯ E B

Em

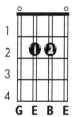

G E B E

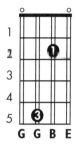

G G B E

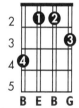

B E B G

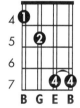

B G E B

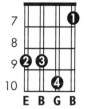

E B G B

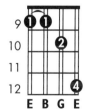

E B G E

E

E°

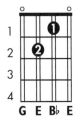

G E B♭ E

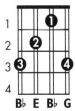

B♭ E B♭ G

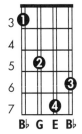

B♭ G E B♭

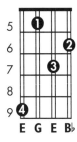

E G E B♭

E

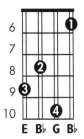

E B♭ G B♭

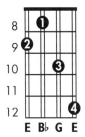

E B♭ G E

E+

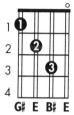

G# E B# E

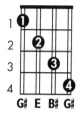

G# E B# G#

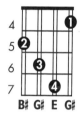

B# G# E G#

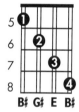

B# G# E B#

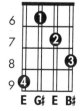

E G# E B#

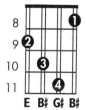

E B# G# B#

E

E5

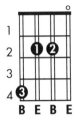

B E B E

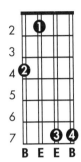

B E E B

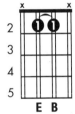

E B

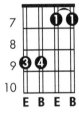

E B E B

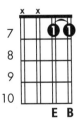

E B

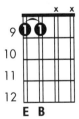

E B

E

Esus4

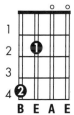

B E A E

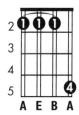

A E B A

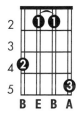

B E B A

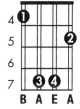

B A E A

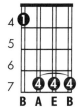

B A E B

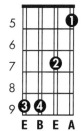

E B E A

E

E6

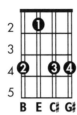

B E C# G#

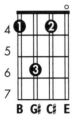

B G# C# E

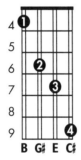

B G# E C#

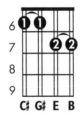

C# G# E B

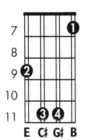

E C# G# B

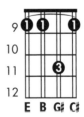

E B G# C#

E

Em6

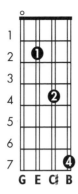

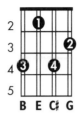

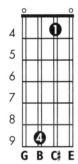

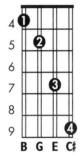

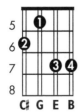

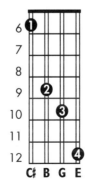

E

Emaj7

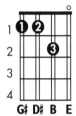

G♯ D♯ B E

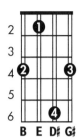

B E D♯ G♯

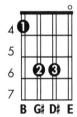

B G♯ D♯ E

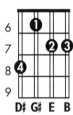

D♯ G♯ E B

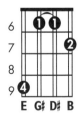

E G♯ D♯ B

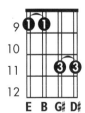

E B G♯ D♯

E

E7

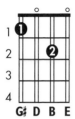

G# D B E

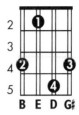

B E D G#

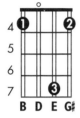

B D E G#

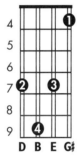

D B E G#

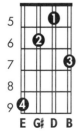

E G# D B

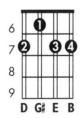

D G# E B

E

Em7

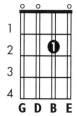

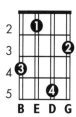

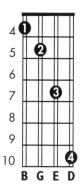

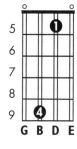

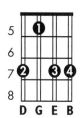

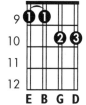

E

Em7(♭5)

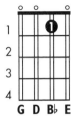

G D B♭ E

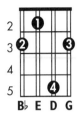

B♭ E D G

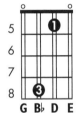

G B♭ D E

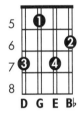

D G E B♭

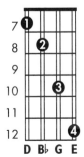

D B♭ G E

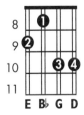

E B♭ G D

E

E°7

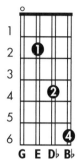

G E Db Bb

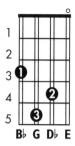

Bb G Db E

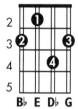

Bb E Db G

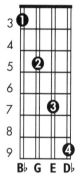

Bb G E Db

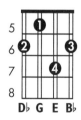

Db G E Bb

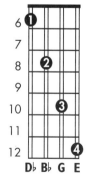

Db Bb G E

E

E(add9)

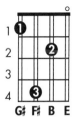

G# F# B E

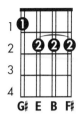

G# E B F#

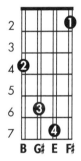

B G# E F#

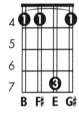

B F# E G#

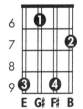

E G# F# B

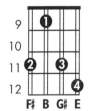

F# B G# E

E

Emaj9

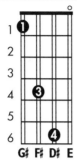
G# F# D# E

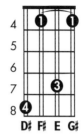
D# F# E G#

E9

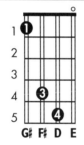
G# F# D E

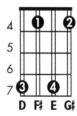
D F# E G#

E

Em9

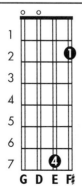
G D E F#

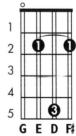
G E D F#

164

E7+

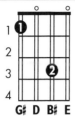

G# D B# E

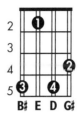

B# E D G#

E7(♭9)

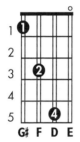

G# F D E

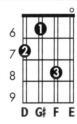

D G# F E

E7(♯9)

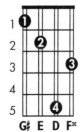

G# E D F✻

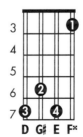

D G# E F✻

E

F

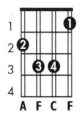

A F C F

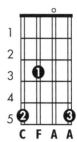

C F A A

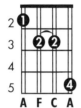

A F C A

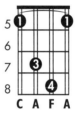

C A F A

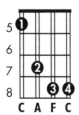

C A F C

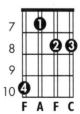

F A F C

Fm

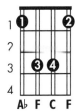

Ab F C F

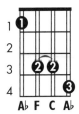

Ab F C Ab

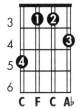

C F C Ab

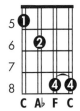

C Ab F C

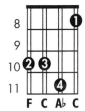

F C Ab C

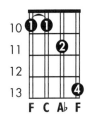

F C Ab F

F

F°

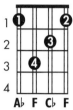

1 Ab
2 F
3 Cb
4 F

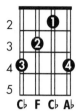

2
3
4
5
Cb F Cb Ab

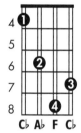

4
5
6
7
8
Cb Ab F Cb

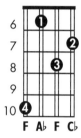

6
7
8
9
10
F Ab F Cb

F

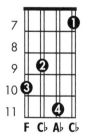

7
8
9
10
11
F Cb Ab Cb

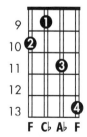

9
10
11
12
13
F Cb Ab F

F+

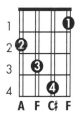

A F C# F

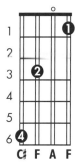

C# F A F

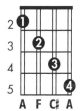

A F C# A

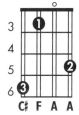

C# F A A

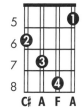

C# A F A

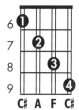

C# A F C#

F5

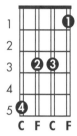

C F C F

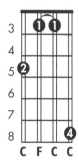

C F C C

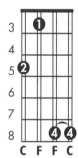

C F F C

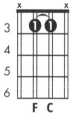

F C

F

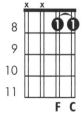

F C

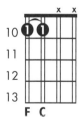

F C

Fsus4

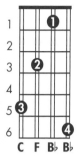

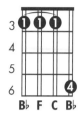

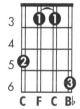

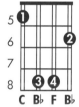

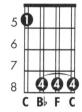

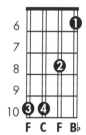

F

F6

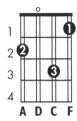

A D C F

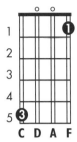

C D A F

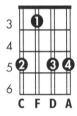

C F D A

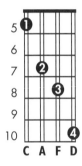

C A F D

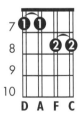

D A F C

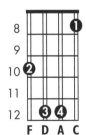

F D A C

F

Fm6

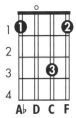

Ab D C F

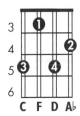

C F D Ab

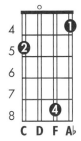

C D F Ab

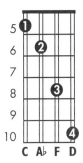

C Ab F D

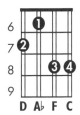

D Ab F C

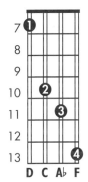

D C Ab F

F

173

Fmaj7

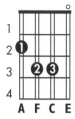

A F C E

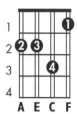

A E C F

C F A E

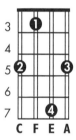

C F E A

F

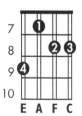

E A F C

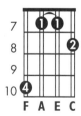

F A E C

F7

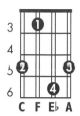

C F E♭ A

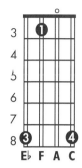

E♭ F A C

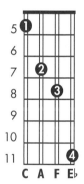

C A F E♭

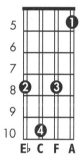

E♭ C F A

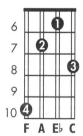

F A E♭ C

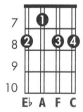

E♭ A F C

F

175

Fm7

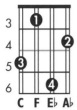

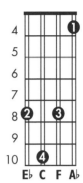

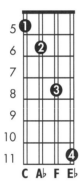

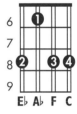

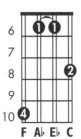

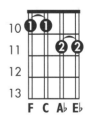

Fm7(♭5)

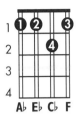

A♭ E♭ C♭ F

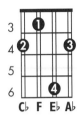

C♭ F E♭ A♭

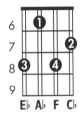

E♭ A♭ F C♭

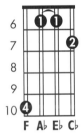

F A♭ E♭ C♭

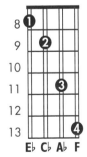

E♭ C♭ A♭ F

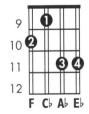

F C♭ A♭ E♭

F

F°7

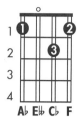

Ab Eb Cb F

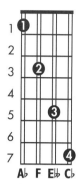

Ab F Eb Cb

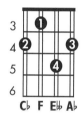

Cb F Eb Ab

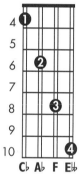

Cb Ab F Eb

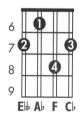

Eb Ab F Cb

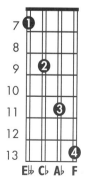

Eb Cb Ab F

F(add9)

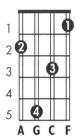

A G C F

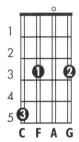

C F A G

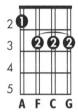

A F C G

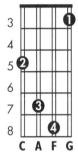

C A F G

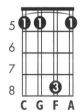

C G F A

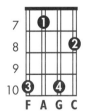

F A G C

Fmaj9

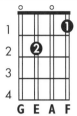

F9

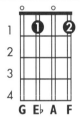
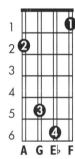

Fm9

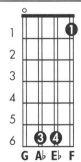
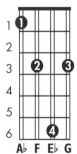

F

F7+

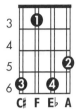

C# F E♭ A

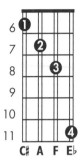

C# A F E♭

F7(♭9)

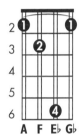

A F E♭ G♭

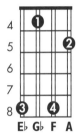

E♭ G♭ F A

F7(#9)

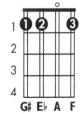

G# E♭ A F

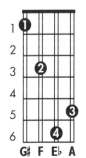

G# F E♭ A

F

181

F#

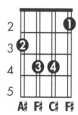

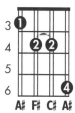

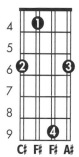

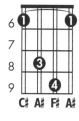

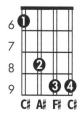

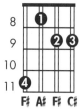

F#

F#m

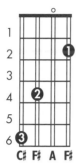

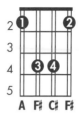

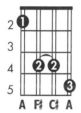

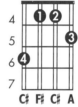

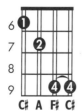

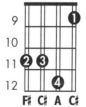

F#

F#°

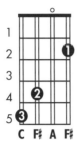

C F# A F#

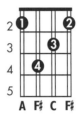

A F# C F#

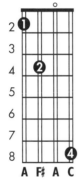

A F# A C

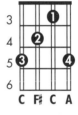

C F# C A

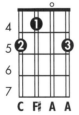

C F# A A

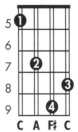

C A F# C

F#

F#+

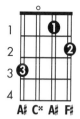

A# C* A# F#

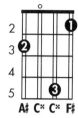

A# C* C* F#

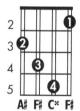

A# F# C* F#

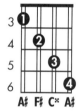

A# F# C* A#

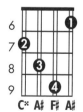

C* A# F# A#

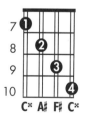

C* A# F# C*

F#5

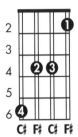

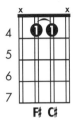

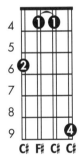

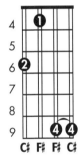

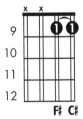

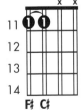

F#

F#sus4

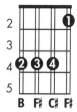

B F# C# F#

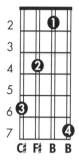

C# F# B B

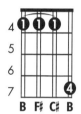

B F# C# B

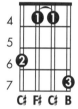

C# F# C# B

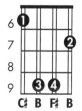

C# B F# B

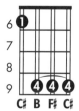

C# B F# C#

187

F#6

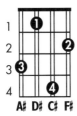

A# D# C# F#

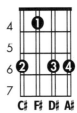

C# F# D# A#

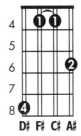

D# F# C# A#

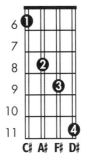

C# A# F# D#

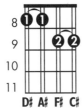

D# A# F# C#

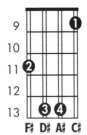

F# D# A# C#

F#

188

F#m6

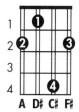

A D# C# F#

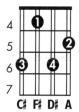

C# F# D# A

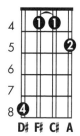

D# F# C# A

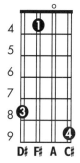

D# F# A C#

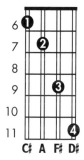

C# A F# D#

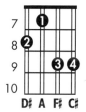

D# A F# C#

F#maj7

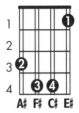

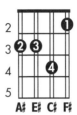

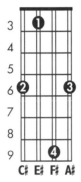

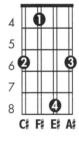

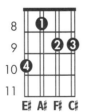

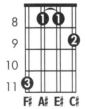

F#7

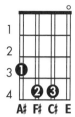

A# F# C# E

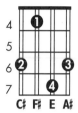

C# F# E A#

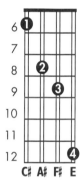

C# A# F# E

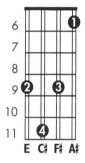

E C# F# A#

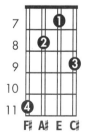

F# A# E C#

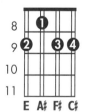

E A# F# C#

F#

F#m7

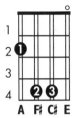

A F# C# E

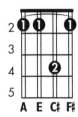

A E C# F#

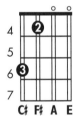

C# F# A E

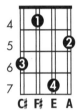

C# F# E A

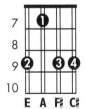

E A F# C#

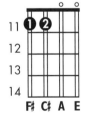

F# C# A E

F#

F#m7(♭5)

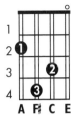

A F# C E

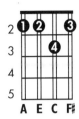

A E C F#

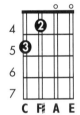

C F# A E

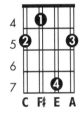

C F# E A

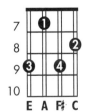

E A F# C

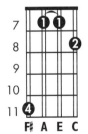

F# A E C

F#

F#°7

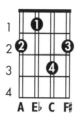

A E♭ C F#

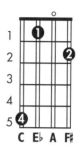

C E♭ A F#

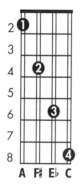

A F# E♭ C

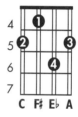

C F# E♭ A

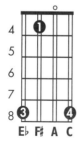

E♭ F# A C

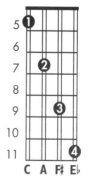

C A F# E♭

F#

F#(add9)

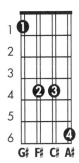

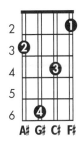

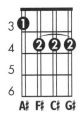

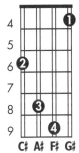

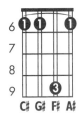

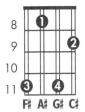

F#

F#maj9

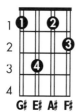
G# E# A# F#

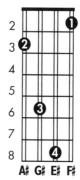
A# G# E# F#

F#9

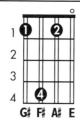
G# F# A# E

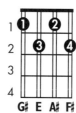
G# E A# F#

F#m9

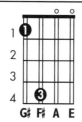
G# F# A E

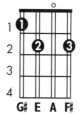
G# E A F#

F#

F#7+

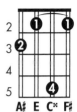
A# E C× F#

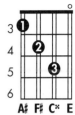
A# F# C× E

F#7(♭9)

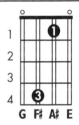
G F# A# E

G E A# F#

F#7(#9)

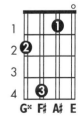
G× F# A# E

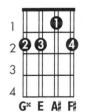
G× E A# F#

F#

197

G

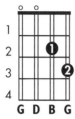

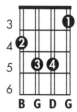

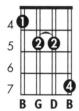

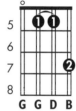

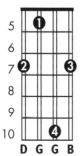

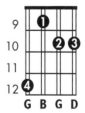

Gm

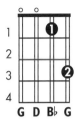

G D B♭ G

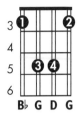

B♭ G D G

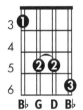

B♭ G D B♭

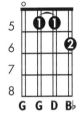

G G D B♭

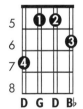

D G D B♭

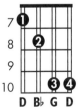

D B♭ G D

G

G°

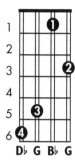

Db G Bb G

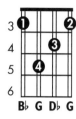

Bb G Db G

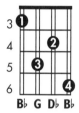

Bb G Db Bb

G G Db Bb

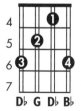

Db G Db Bb

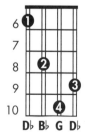

Db Bb G Db

G

G+

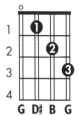

G D# B G

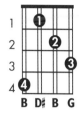

B D# B G

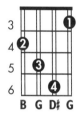

B G D# G

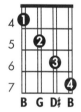

B G D# B

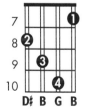

D# B G B

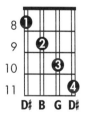

D# B G D#

G

G5

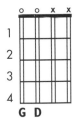

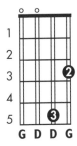

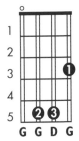

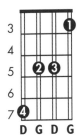

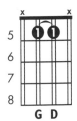

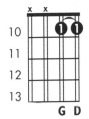

G

Gsus4

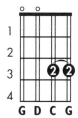

G D C G

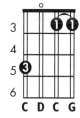

C D C G

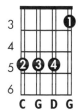

C G D G

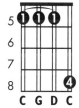

C G D C

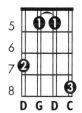

D G D C

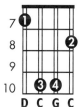

D C G C

G

203

G6

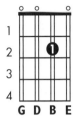

G D B E

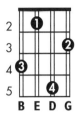

B E D G

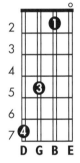

D G B E

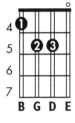

B G D E

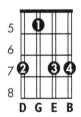

D G E B

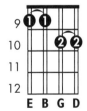

E B G D

G

204

Gm6

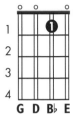

G D B♭ E

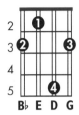

B♭ E D G

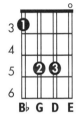

B♭ G D E

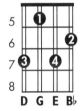

D G E B♭

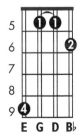

E G D B♭

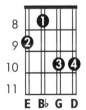

E B♭ G D

G

Gmaj7

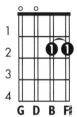

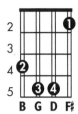

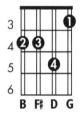

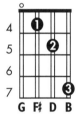

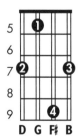

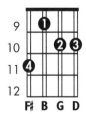

G

206

G7

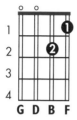

G D B F

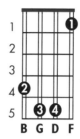

B G D F

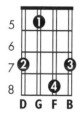

D G F B

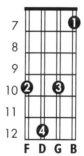

F D G B

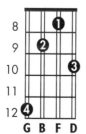

G B F D

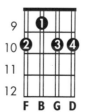

F B G D

G

Gm7

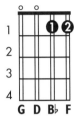
G D B♭ F

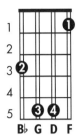
B♭ G D F

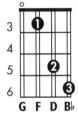
G F D B♭

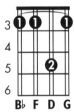
B♭ F D G

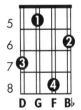
D G F B♭

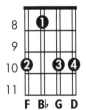
F B♭ G D

Gm7(♭5)

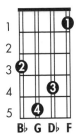

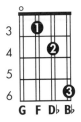

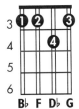

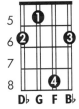

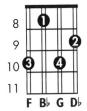

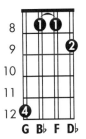

G

G°7

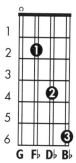

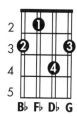

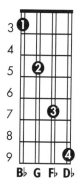

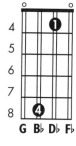

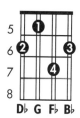

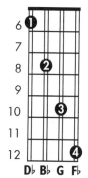

G

210

G(add9)

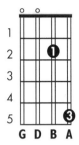

G D B A

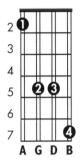

A G D B

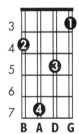

B A D G

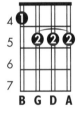

B G D A

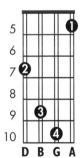

D B G A

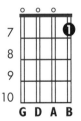

G D A B

G

Gmaj9

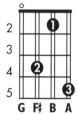

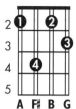

G9

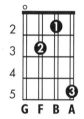

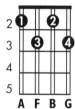

Gm9

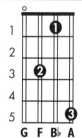

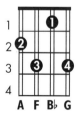

G

G7+

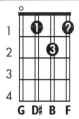

G D# B F

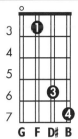

G F D# B

G7(♭9)

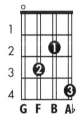

G F B A♭

G A♭ B F

G7(♯9)

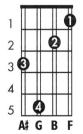

A♯ G B F

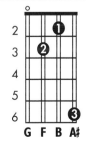

G F B A♯

G

213

Moveable Chords

Definitions

These chords are called "moveable" because once a single fingering form is learned, it can be moved up and down the fingerboard. With moveable chord forms, a single fingering can be used for as many as 12 different chords.

A *barre* means to hold down two or more strings using only one finger. If the finger holds down all four strings, the barre is called "full."

Roots and Moveable Chords

Every chord has a root. As we learned on page 9, the root is the note that names the chord. For example, the root of an E Major chord is the note E, the root of an A Minor chord is the note A, the root of a C7 chord is the note C, and so on.

With moveable chords, it is important to remember that, regardless of the fret on which the chord is played, the root always remains on the same string.

In the example on the right, the root of the A Major chord is A. This note is found on the 4th string.

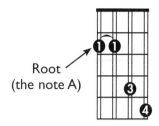

Root
(the note A)

Since the name of the note on the 4th string is A, and since we started with a moveable form of a major chord, the name of this chord is A Major. If we move the chord up one more fret, the root is still found on the 4th string. The note is B♭ and the chord is now B♭ Major.

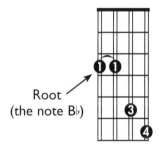

Root
(the note B♭)

In the following pages, you will learn how to play nine different types of moveable chords, each of which has a fingering with the root on the 4th string, 3rd string, and 2nd string. So, in total, you will learn 27 different fingerings.

By applying the same method discussed above, you can play 12 different chords with each fingering. Multiply 12 by 27 (the total number of fingerings in this section) and you have 324—the number of chords you will be able to play by learning only 27 fingerings and the notes on the fingerboard.

NOTE: To review the notes on the fingerboard, you can refer to the illustration on page 232.

Moveable Major Chord

Moveable Major Chord—Root on the 4th String

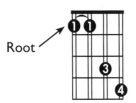

With Root At:		
1st Fret	=	A♭ (G♯)
2nd Fret	=	A
3rd Fret	=	B♭ (A♯)
4th Fret	=	B
5th Fret	=	C
6th Fret	=	C♯ (D♭)
7th Fret	=	D
8th Fret	=	E♭ (D♯)
9th Fret	=	E
10th Fret	=	F
11th Fret	=	F♯ (G♭)
12th Fret	=	G

Moveable Major Chord—Root on the 3rd String

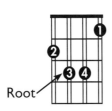

With Root At:		
3rd Fret	=	F
4th Fret	=	F♯ (G♭)
5th Fret	=	G
6th Fret	=	A♭ (G♯)
7th Fret	=	A
8th Fret	=	B♭ (A♯)
9th Fret	=	B
10th Fret	=	C
11th Fret	=	C♯ (D♭)
12th Fret	=	D
13th Fret	=	E♭ (D♯)
14th Fret	=	E

Moveable Major Chord—Root on the 2nd String

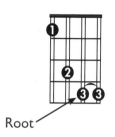

Root

With Root At:		
4th Fret	=	C♯ (D♭)
5th Fret	=	D
6th Fret	=	E♭ (D♯)
7th Fret	=	E
8th Fret	=	F
9th Fret	=	F♯ (G♭)
10th Fret	=	G
11th Fret	=	A♭ (G♯)
12th Fret	=	A
13th Fret	=	B♭ (A♯)
14th Fret	=	B
15th Fret	=	C

Moveable Minor Chord
Moveable Minor Chord—Root on the 4th String

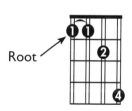

Root

With Root At:		
1st Fret	=	A♭m (G♯m)
2nd Fret	=	Am
3rd Fret	=	B♭m (A♯m)
4th Fret	=	Bm
5th Fret	=	Cm
6th Fret	=	C♯m (D♭m)
7th Fret	=	Dm
8th Fret	=	E♭m (D♯m)
9th Fret	=	Em
10th Fret	=	Fm
11th Fret	=	F♯m (G♭m)
12th Fret	=	Gm

Moveable Minor Chord—Root on the 3rd String

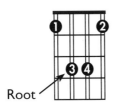

Root

With Root At:		
3rd Fret	=	Fm
4th Fret	=	F#m (G♭m)
5th Fret	=	Gm
6th Fret	=	A♭m (G#m)
7th Fret	=	Am
8th Fret	=	B♭m (A#m)
9th Fret	=	Bm
10th Fret	=	Cm
11th Fret	=	C#m (D♭m)
12th Fret	=	Dm
13th Fret	=	E♭m (D#m)
14th Fret	=	Em

Moveable Minor Chord—Root on the 2nd String

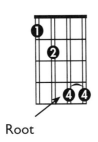

Root

With Root At:		
4th Fret	=	C#m (D♭m)
5th Fret	=	Dm
6th Fret	=	E♭m (D#m)
7th Fret	=	Em
8th Fret	=	Fm
9th Fret	=	F#m (G♭m)
10th Fret	=	Gm
11th Fret	=	A♭m (G#m)
12th Fret	=	Am
13th Fret	=	B♭m (A#m)
14th Fret	=	Bm
15th Fret	=	Cm

Moveable 5th Chord
Moveable 5th Chord—Root on the 4th String

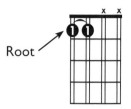

Root

With Root At:		
1st Fret	=	A♭5 (G♯5)
2nd Fret	=	A5
3rd Fret	=	B♭5 (A♯5)
4th Fret	=	B5
5th Fret	=	C5
6th Fret	=	C♯5 (D♭5)
7th Fret	=	D5
8th Fret	=	E♭5 (D♯5)
9th Fret	=	E5
10th Fret	=	F5
11th Fret	=	F♯5 (G♭5)
12th Fret	=	G5

Moveable 5th Chord—Root on the 3rd String

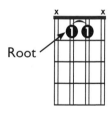

Root

With Root At:		
1st Fret	=	E♭5 (D♯5)
2nd Fret	=	E5
3rd Fret	=	F5
4th Fret	=	F♯5 (G♭5)
5th Fret	=	G5
6th Fret	=	A♭5 (G♯5)
7th Fret	=	A5
8th Fret	=	B♭5 (A♯5)
9th Fret	=	B5
10th Fret	=	C5
11th Fret	=	C♯5 (D♭5)
12th Fret	=	D5

Moveable 5th Chord—Root on the 2nd String

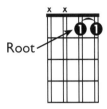

Root

With Root At:		
1st Fret	=	B♭5 (A♯5)
2nd Fret	=	B5
3rd Fret	=	C5
4th Fret	=	C♯5 (D♭5)
5th Fret	=	D5
6th Fret	=	E♭5 (D♯5)
7th Fret	=	E5
8th Fret	=	F5
9th Fret	=	F♯5 (G♭5)
10th Fret	=	G5
11th Fret	=	A♭5 (G♯5)
12th Fret	=	A5

Moveable 6th Chord
Moveable 6th Chord—Root on the 4th String

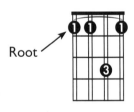

Root

With Root At:		
1st Fret	=	A♭6 (G♯6)
2nd Fret	=	A6
3rd Fret	=	B♭6 (A♯6)
4th Fret	=	B6
5th Fret	=	C6
6th Fret	=	C♯6 (D♭6)
7th Fret	=	D6
8th Fret	=	E♭6 (D♯6)
9th Fret	=	E6
10th Fret	=	F6
11th Fret	=	F♯6 (G♭6)
12th Fret	=	G6

Moveable 6th Chord—Root on the 3rd String

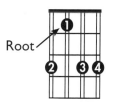

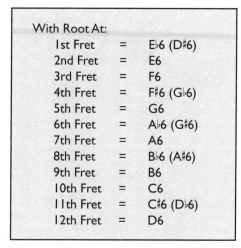

With Root At:		
1st Fret	=	E♭6 (D♯6)
2nd Fret	=	E6
3rd Fret	=	F6
4th Fret	=	F♯6 (G♭6)
5th Fret	=	G6
6th Fret	=	A♭6 (G♯6)
7th Fret	=	A6
8th Fret	=	B♭6 (A♯6)
9th Fret	=	B6
10th Fret	=	C6
11th Fret	=	C♯6 (D♭6)
12th Fret	=	D6

Moveable 6th Chord—Root on the 2nd String

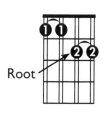

With Root At:		
2nd Fret	=	B6
3rd Fret	=	C6
4th Fret	=	C♯6 (D♭6)
5th Fret	=	D6
6th Fret	=	E♭6 (D♯6)
7th Fret	=	E6
8th Fret	=	F6
9th Fret	=	F♯6 (G♭6)
10th Fret	=	G6
11th Fret	=	A♭6 (G♯6)
12th Fret	=	A6
13th Fret	=	B♭6 (A♯6)

Moveable Minor 6th Chord
Moveable Minor 6th Chord—Root on the 4th String

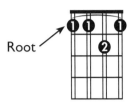

Root

With Root At:		
1st Fret	=	A♭m6 (G♯m6)
2nd Fret	=	Am6
3rd Fret	=	B♭m6 (A♯m6)
4th Fret	=	Bm6
5th Fret	=	Cm6
6th Fret	=	C♯m6 (D♭m6)
7th Fret	=	Dm6
8th Fret	=	E♭m6 (D♯m6)
9th Fret	=	Em6
10th Fret	=	Fm6
11th Fret	=	F♯m6 (G♭m6)
12th Fret	=	Gm6

Moveable Minor 6th Chord—Root on the 3rd String

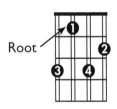

Root

With Root At:		
1st Fret	=	E♭m6 (D♯m6)
2nd Fret	=	Em6
3rd Fret	=	Fm6
4th Fret	=	F♯m6 (G♭m6)
5th Fret	=	Gm6
6th Fret	=	A♭m6 (G♯m6)
7th Fret	=	Am6
8th Fret	=	B♭m6 (A♯m6)
9th Fret	=	Bm6
10th Fret	=	Cm6
11th Fret	=	C♯m6 (D♭m6)
12th Fret	=	Dm6

Moveable Minor 6th Chord—Root on the 2nd String

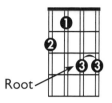

Root

With Root At:		
3rd Fret	=	Cm6
4th Fret	=	C#m6 (D♭m6)
5th Fret	=	Dm6
6th Fret	=	E♭m6 (D#m6)
7th Fret	=	Em6
8th Fret	=	Fm6
9th Fret	=	F#m6 (G♭m6)
10th Fret	=	Gm6
11th Fret	=	A♭m6 (G#m6)
12th Fret	=	Am6
13th Fret	=	B♭m6 (A#m6)
14th Fret	=	Bm6

Moveable 7th Chord
Moveable 7th Chord—Root on the 4th String

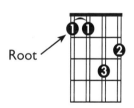

Root

With Root At:		
1st Fret	=	A♭7 (G#7)
2nd Fret	=	A7
3rd Fret	=	B♭7 (A#7)
4th Fret	=	B7
5th Fret	=	C7
6th Fret	=	C#7 (D♭7)
7th Fret	=	D7
8th Fret	=	E♭7 (D#7)
9th Fret	=	E7
10th Fret	=	F7
11th Fret	=	F#7 (G♭7)
12th Fret	=	G7

Moveable 7th Chord—Root on the 3rd String

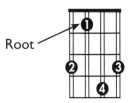

Root

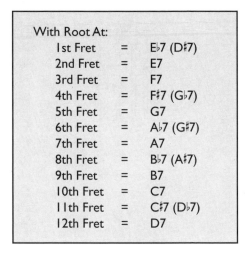

With Root At:

1st Fret	=	E♭7 (D♯7)
2nd Fret	=	E7
3rd Fret	=	F7
4th Fret	=	F♯7 (G♭7)
5th Fret	=	G7
6th Fret	=	A♭7 (G♯7)
7th Fret	=	A7
8th Fret	=	B♭7 (A♯7)
9th Fret	=	B7
10th Fret	=	C7
11th Fret	=	C♯7 (D♭7)
12th Fret	=	D7

Moveable 7th Chord—Root on the 2nd String

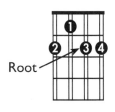

Root

With Root At:

2nd Fret	=	B7
3rd Fret	=	C7
4th Fret	=	C♯7 (D♭7)
5th Fret	=	D7
6th Fret	=	E♭7 (D♯7)
7th Fret	=	E7
8th Fret	=	F7
9th Fret	=	F♯7 (G♭7)
10th Fret	=	G7
11th Fret	=	A♭7 (G♯7)
12th Fret	=	A7
13th Fret	=	B♭7 (A♯7)

Moveable Major 7th Chord
Moveable Major 7th Chord—Root on the 4th String

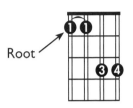

Root

With Root At:		
1st Fret	=	A♭maj7 (G♯maj7)
2nd Fret	=	Amaj7
3rd Fret	=	B♭maj7 (A♯maj7)
4th Fret	=	Bmaj7
5th Fret	=	Cmaj7
6th Fret	=	C♯maj7 (D♭maj7)
7th Fret	=	Dmaj7
8th Fret	=	E♭maj7 (D♯maj7)
9th Fret	=	Emaj7
10th Fret	=	Fmaj7
11th Fret	=	F♯maj7 (G♭maj7)
12th Fret	=	Gmaj7

Moveable Major 7th Chord—Root on the 3rd String

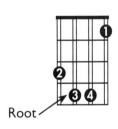

Root

With Root At:		
4th Fret	=	F♯maj7 (G♭maj7)
5th Fret	=	Gmaj7
6th Fret	=	A♭maj7 (G♯maj7)
7th Fret	=	Amaj7
8th Fret	=	B♭maj7 (A♯maj7)
9th Fret	=	Bmaj7
10th Fret	=	Cmaj7
11th Fret	=	C♯maj7 (D♭maj7)
12th Fret	=	Dmaj7
13th Fret	=	E♭maj7 (D♯maj7)
14th Fret	=	Emaj7
15th Fret	=	Fmaj7

Moveable Major 7th Chord—Root on the 2nd String

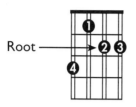

Root ⟶

With Root At:		
2nd Fret	=	Bmaj7
3rd Fret	=	Cmaj7
4th Fret	=	C#maj7 (D♭maj7)
5th Fret	=	Dmaj7
6th Fret	=	E♭maj7 (D#maj7)
7th Fret	=	Emaj7
8th Fret	=	Fmaj7
9th Fret	=	F#maj7 (G♭maj7)
10th Fret	=	Gmaj7
11th Fret	=	A♭maj7 (G#maj7)
12th Fret	=	Amaj7
13th Fret	=	B♭maj7 (A#maj7)

Moveable Minor 7th Chord
Moveable Minor 7th Chord—Root on the 4th String

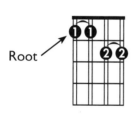

Root ⟶

With Root At:		
1st Fret	=	A♭m7 (G#m7)
2nd Fret	=	Am7
3rd Fret	=	B♭m7 (A#m7)
4th Fret	=	Bm7
5th Fret	=	Cm7
6th Fret	=	C#m7 (D♭m7)
7th Fret	=	Dm7
8th Fret	=	E♭m7 (D#m7)
9th Fret	=	Em7
10th Fret	=	Fm7
11th Fret	=	F#m7 (G♭m7)
12th Fret	=	Gm7

Moveable Minor 7th Chord—Root on the 3rd String

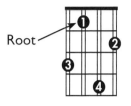

With Root At:		
1st Fret	=	E♭m7 (D♯m7)
2nd Fret	=	Em7
3rd Fret	=	Fm7
4th Fret	=	F♯m7 (G♭m7)
5th Fret	=	Gm7
6th Fret	=	A♭m7 (G♯m7)
7th Fret	=	Am7
8th Fret	=	B♭m7 (A♯m7)
9th Fret	=	Bm7
10th Fret	=	Cm7
11th Fret	=	C♯m7 (D♭m7)
12th Fret	=	Dm7

Moveable Minor 7th Chord—Root on the 2nd String

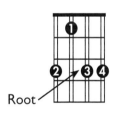

With Root At:		
3rd Fret	=	Cm7
4th Fret	=	C♯m7 (D♭m7)
5th Fret	=	Dm7
6th Fret	=	E♭m7 (D♯m7)
7th Fret	=	Em7
8th Fret	=	Fm7
9th Fret	=	F♯m7 (G♭m7)
10th Fret	=	Gm7
11th Fret	=	A♭m7 (G♯m7)
12th Fret	=	Am7
13th Fret	=	B♭m7 (A♯m7)
14th Fret	=	Bm7

Moveable 9th Chord
Moveable 9th Chord—Root on the 4th String

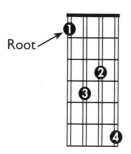

Root

With Root At:		
1st Fret	=	A♭9 (G♯9)
2nd Fret	=	A9
3rd Fret	=	B♭9 (A♯9)
4th Fret	=	B9
5th Fret	=	C9
6th Fret	=	C♯9 (D♭9)
7th Fret	=	D9
8th Fret	=	E♭9 (D♯9)
9th Fret	=	E9
10th Fret	=	F9
11th Fret	=	F♯9 (G♭9)
12th Fret	=	G9

Moveable 9th Chord—Root on the 3rd String

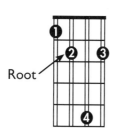

Root

With Root At:		
2nd Fret	=	E9
3rd Fret	=	F9
4th Fret	=	F♯9 (G♭9)
5th Fret	=	G9
6th Fret	=	A♭9 (G♯9)
7th Fret	=	A9
8th Fret	=	B♭9 (A♯9)
9th Fret	=	B9
10th Fret	=	C9
11th Fret	=	C♯9 (D♭9)
12th Fret	=	D9
13th Fret	=	E♭9 (D♯9)

Moveable 9th Chord—Root on the 2nd String

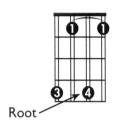

Root

With Root At:		
4th Fret	=	C♯9 (D♭9)
5th Fret	=	D9
6th Fret	=	E♭9 (D♯9)
7th Fret	=	E9
8th Fret	=	F9
9th Fret	=	F♯9 (G♭9)
10th Fret	=	G9
11th Fret	=	A♭9 (G♯9)
12th Fret	=	A9
13th Fret	=	B♭9 (A♯9)
14th Fret	=	B9
15th Fret	=	C9

Moveable Minor 9th Chord
Moveable Minor 9th Chord—Root on the 4th String

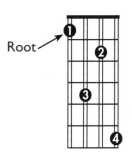

Root

With Root At:		
1st Fret	=	A♭m9 (G♯m9)
2nd Fret	=	Am9
3rd Fret	=	B♭m9 (A♯m9)
4th Fret	=	Bm9
5th Fret	=	Cm9
6th Fret	=	C♯m9 (D♭m9)
7th Fret	=	Dm9
8th Fret	=	E♭m9 (D♯m9)
9th Fret	=	Em9
10th Fret	=	Fm9
11th Fret	=	F♯m9 (G♭m9)
12th Fret	=	Gm9

Moveable Minor 9th Chord—Root on the 3rd String

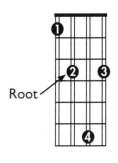

Root

With Root At:		
3rd Fret	=	Fm9
4th Fret	=	F♯m9 (G♭m9)
5th Fret	=	Gm9
6th Fret	=	A♭m9 (G♯m9)
7th Fret	=	Am9
8th Fret	=	B♭m9 (A♯m9)
9th Fret	=	Bm9
10th Fret	=	Cm9
11th Fret	=	C♯m9 (D♭m9)
12th Fret	=	Dm9
13th Fret	=	E♭m9 (D♯m9)
14th Fret	=	Em9